The Voices of Marrakesh

ELIAS CANETTI

The Voices of Marrakesh

A Record of a Visit

TRANSLATED FROM THE GERMAN BY
J. A. UNDERWOOD

CONTINUUM • NEW YORK

The Continuum Publishing Corporation
575 Lexington Avenue
New York, N.Y. 10022

Originally published as *Die Stimmen von Marrakesch*
by Carl Hanser Verlag, copyright © 1967 by Elias Canetti.

English translation copyright © 1978 by
Marion Boyars Publishers Ltd.

Printed in the United States of America

Library of Congress Cataloging In Publication Data

Canetti, Elias, 1905–
The voices of Marrakesh.

Translation of: Die Stimmen von Marrakesch.
Reprint. Originally published:
New York: Seabury Press, 1978.
1. Marrakesh (Morocco)—Description.
2. Canetti, Elias, 1905–   . 3. Title
DT329.M3C313   1981   916.4'6   81-17519
ISBN 0-8264-0170-8   AACR2
ISBN 0-8264-0213-5 (pbk.)

Contents

For Veza Canetti

The Voices of Marrakesh

Encounters with camels

I came into contact with camels on three occasions, and each occasion ended tragically.

'I must show you the camel market,' said my friend soon after my arrival in Marrakesh. 'It's held every Thursday morning by the wall near the Bab-el-Khemis. That's right on the other side of the city – I'd better drive you there.'

Thursday came and we drove there. We had started late, and by the time we reached the large open square by the city wall it was already noon. The square was almost empty. At the far end, about two hundred yards from us, stood a group of people, but we could see no camels. The little animals these people were occupied with were donkeys, and the city was full of donkeys anyway; they carried all the burdens and were so badly treated we certainly had no desire to see any more of it. 'We're too late,' said my friend. 'The camel market's over.' He drove into the middle of the square to convince me that there was really nothing more to be seen.

But before he stopped we saw a knot of people scatter. In their midst, balanced on three legs, its fourth having been bound up, stood a camel. It was wearing a red muzzle. A rope had been threaded through its nostrils and a man standing at some distance was trying to pull the animal away. It ran forwards a little way, stopped, and then made a surprising leap into the air on its three legs. Its movements were as unexpected as they were uncanny. The man who was supposed to be leading it gave way every time; he was afraid to approach too close to the animal, never quite sure what it would get up to next. But he drew the rope tight again after each surprise, and he did manage very slowly to drag the animal in a particular direction.

We stopped and wound down the windows of the car; begging children surrounded us, and above their voices as they asked for alms we could hear the camel shrieking. Once it jumped so violently to one side that the man who was leading it lost his hold on the rope. The onlookers, who were standing at some distance, ran off even farther. The air around the camel was charged with fear, most of it coming from the camel itself. The drover ran with it for a bit and snatched up the rope as it trailed along the ground. The camel leaped sideways into the air with an undulating movement but did not break loose again; it was dragged along farther.

A man we had not noticed appeared behind the children standing around our car, pushed them aside, and explained to us in broken French: 'The camel has rabies. It is dangerous. It is being taken to the slaughterhouse. One has to be very careful.' He pulled a serious face. Between each of his sentences we could hear the animal's shrieks.

We thanked him and drove away saddened. We often spoke of the rabid camel during the next few days; its despairing movements had made a deep impression on us.

We had gone to the market expecting to see hundreds of these gentle, curvaceous beasts. But in that huge square we had found only one, on three legs, captive, living its last hour, and as it fought for its life we had driven away.

Some days later we were passing another part of the city wall. It was evening; the red glow on the wall was beginning to fade. I kept the wall in view for as long as I could, delighting in the way its colouring gradually changed. Then, in the shadow of the wall, I saw a large caravan of camels. Most of them had lowered themselves to their knees; others were still standing. Men with turbans on their heads went busily and yet quietly about among them. It was a picture of peace and twilight. The camels' colouring blended with that of the wall. We got out of the car and walked among the animals ourselves. They knelt in rings of a dozen or more around mountainous piles of fodder. They stretched their necks out, drew the fodder into their mouths, threw their heads back, and calmly worked their jaws. We looked at them closely and I tell you they had faces. They all looked alike and yet they were so different. They put one in mind of elderly English ladies taking tea together, dignified and apparently bored but unable entirely to conceal the malice with which they observe everything around them: 'That one's my aunt, honestly,' said my English friend when I tactfully pointed out this resemblance to his countrywomen, and we soon spotted other acquaintances. We were proud of having come across this caravan that no one had told us about, and we counted 107 camels.

A young lad aproached us and asked us for a coin. His face was dark blue in colour, as was his robe; he was a drover and, to judge from his appearance, one of the so-called 'blue men' who live to the south of the Atlas. The dye in their clothing, we had been told, comes off on their skin, making them all, men and women, blue – the only blue race. Our young drover was grateful for the coin and we tried to find out from him something about the caravan. He knew only a few words of French, however: they were from Goulimime and they had been on the road for twenty-five days. That was all we understood. Goulimime was in the desert away down to the south, and we wondered whether the camel caravan had crossed the Atlas. We would also have liked to know where it was going, because here beneath the walls of the city could hardly be its journey's end and the animals appeared to be fortifying themselves for exertions to come.

The dark-blue lad, unable to tell us any more, went out of his way to be helpful by leading us to a tall, slender old man who wore a white turban and was treated with respect. He spoke French well and answered our questions fluently. The caravan was from Goulimime and really had been on the road for twenty-five days.

'And where is it going from here?'

'Nowhere,' he said. 'They will be sold here for slaughter.'

'For slaughter?'

We were both of us shocked – even my friend, who at home is an enthusiastic hunter. We thought of the long journey the animals had behind them; of their beauty in the dusk; of their ignorance of what lay in store for them; of their peaceful meal; and perhaps, too, of the people they had reminded us of.

'Yes, for slaughter,' the old man repeated. His voice had a jagged quality, like the edge of a blunted knife.

'Do people eat a lot of camel meat here then?' I asked, trying with matter-of-fact questions to conceal how shocked I was.

'Masses of it!'

'What does it taste like? I've never had any.'

'You've never had camel meat?' He broke into a thin, derisive chuckle and said again, 'You've never had camel meat?' Clearly he believed we were given nothing but camel meat, and he put on a very superior air as if we were eating it as his bidding. 'It's very good,' he said.

'What does a camel cost?'

'It varies a great deal. Anything from 30,000 to 70,000 francs. Here – I can show you. You have to know what you're doing.' He led us over to a very beautiful, light-coloured animal and touched it with his stick, which I noticed now for the first time. 'This is a good animal. This one is worth 70,000 francs. The owner rode it himself. He could have gone on using it for years. But he preferred to sell it. With the money, you see, he can buy two young animals.'

We saw. 'Are you from Goulimime – did you come with the caravan?' I asked.

He rejected this suggestion in some annoyance. 'I am from Marrakesh,' he said proudly. 'I buy animals and sell them to the butchers.' He had nothing but scorn for the men who had come all that way, and our young drover he dismissed with the words: 'He doesn't know a thing.'

But he wanted to know where we were from, and we told him for the sake of simplicity that we were both 'from London'. He smiled and appeared to be slightly nettled. 'I was in France during the war,' he said. His age made it plain he was talking of the First World War.

'I was with Englishmen. I didn't get on with them,' he added quickly, dropping his voice a little. 'But war isn't war any more. It's not the man that counts nowadays – it's the machine.' He said some more things about war that sounded very resigned. 'It isn't war any more.' We agreed with him on this point and it seemed to help him get over the fact that we were from England.

'Are all the animals sold already?' I asked.

'No. They can't sell them all. The rest stay with them and go on to Settat. Do you know Settat? It's on the way to Casablanca, 160 kilometres from here. That's the last camel market. The rest will be sold there.'

We thanked him and he dismissed us without ceremony. We stopped walking round among the camels; we did not feel like it any more. It was almost dark when we left the caravan.

But the sight of those camels would not leave me. I thought of them with aversion, and yet it was as if they were something I had long been familiar with. The memory of their last meal merged with that conversation about war. The idea of visiting the next camel market remained with us till the Thursday. We determined to set out early in the morning, and possibly we hoped to gain a less sombre impression of camel existence this time.

We came to the El-Khemis Gate. The number of animals we found there was none too great; they were lost in the expanse of the square, which would have been difficult to fill. On one side were the donkeys again. We did not go over to them but stayed with the camels. There were never more than three or four of them together at a time; sometimes there was just one young animal standing beside its mother. At first they all seemed to be quiet. The only sound came from small groups of men haggling fiercely. Yet it struck me that the men apparently did not trust certain of the animals; these they avoided approaching too closely except when they absolutely had to.

It was not long before our attention was drawn to a camel that appeared to be putting up some kind of resistance; it was grunting and growling and flinging its head about in all directions. A man was trying to force it to its knees, and because it would not obey he was backing up his efforts with blows of his stick. Of the two or three other people busying themselves at the animal's head one stood out particularly: a powerful, stocky man with a dark, cruel face. His stance was solid, his legs as if rooted in the ground. With brisk movements of his arms he was drawing a rope through a hole he had bored in the animal's septum. Nose and rope were red with blood. The camel flinched and shrieked, now and then uttering a great roar; finally it leaped to its feet again, having by now knelt down, and tried to tug itself free, while the man pulled the rope tighter and tighter. The others made a supreme effort to control the animal, and they were still at it when someone came up to us and said in broken French:

'It smells. It can smell the butcher. It has been sold for slaughter. It is going now to the slaughterhouse.'

'But how can it smell that?' asked my friend, incredulous.

'That is the butcher standing in front of him,' and he pointed to the burly, dark fellow who had caught our eye. 'The butcher has come from the slaughterhouse and smells of camel blood. The camel does not like that. A camel can be very dangerous. When one has rabies it comes in the night and kills people in their sleep.'

'How can it kill people?' I asked.

'When they are asleep the camel comes and kneels on them and suffocates them in their sleep. One has to be very careful. Before the people wake up they have suffocated. Oh yes, the camel has a very good nose. It lies beside its master at night and scents thieves and wakes its master up. The meat is good. One should eat camel meat. Ça donne du courage. A camel does not like to be alone. It will go nowhere alone. If a man wants to drive his camel to the city he must find another one to go with it. He must borrow one, otherwise he will never get his camel to the city. It does not want to be alone. I was in the war. I was wounded. Look – here,' and he pointed to his chest.

The camel had calmed down a little and I turned to look at the speaker for the first time. His chest had a caved-in look and his left arm was stiff. The man struck me as familiar. He was small, thin, and very earnest. I wondered where I had seen him before.

'How are camels killed?'

'You sever the jugular vein. They have to bleed to death. Otherwise one is not allowed to eat them. A Moslem is not allowed to eat them unless they have bled to death. I cannot work because of this wound, so I do a bit of guiding here. I spoke to you last Thursday – do you remember the camel with rabies? I was in Safi when the Americans landed. We fought a bit against the Americans, but not much, and then I was taken into the American army. There were a lot of Moroccans in the American army. I was in Corsica and in Italy with the Americans. I went all over the place. The Germans are good soldiers. The Casino was worst. It was really bad there. That's where I got my wound. Do you know the Casino?'

It dawned on me that he meant Monte Cassino. He gave me an account of the fierce fighting there, and in doing so this otherwise calm and self-possessed man became as excited as if it had been a question of the murderous cravings of maddened camels. He was an honest fellow and believed what he said. But he had spotted a group of Americans in among the animals, and he very quickly switched his attentions to them. He disappeared as swiftly as he had appeared, and I had no objection; I had lost sight and sound of the camel, which had now stopped its roaring, and I wanted to see it again.

I soon found it. The butcher had left it where it was. It was kneeling again, still tossing its head from time to time. The blood from its nostrils had spread further. I felt something akin to gratitude for the few illusory moments for which it had been left alone. But I could not look at it for long; I knew its fate and stole away.

My friend had wandered off during the guide's recital in search of some English people he knew. I went looking for him and found him over on the other side of the square, back among the donkeys. Perhaps he felt less uncomfortable there.

During the rest of our stay in the 'red city' we did not mention camels once.

The souks

It is spicy in the souks, and cool and colourful. The smell, always pleasant, changes gradually with the nature of the merchandise. There are no names or signs; there is no glass. Everything for sale is on display. You never know what things will cost; they are neither impaled with their prices, nor are the prices themselves fixed.

All the booths and stalls selling the same thing are close together – twenty or thirty or more of them. There is a bazaar for spices and another for leather goods. The ropemakers have their place and the basketweavers have theirs. Some of the carpet dealers have large, spacious vaults; you stride past them as past a separate city and are meaningly invited inside. The jewellers are grouped round a courtyard of their own, and in many of their narrow booths you can see men at work. You find everything – but you always find it many times over.

The leather handbag you want is on display in twenty different shops, one immediately adjoining another. A man squats among his wares. There is not much room and he has them all close around him. He need hardly stretch to reach every one of his leather handbags, and it is only out of courtesy that, if he is not a very old man, he rises. But the man in the next booth, who looks quite different, sits among the same wares. And it is like that for perhaps a hundred yards, down both sides of the covered passage. It is as if you were being offered all at once everything that this largest and most famous bazaar in the city, indeed in the whole of southern Morocco, possesses in the way of leather goods. There is a great deal of pride in this exhibition. They are showing what they can produce, but they are also showing how much of it there is. The effect is as if the bags themselves knew that they were wealth and were flaunting themselves in their excellence before the eyes of the passers-by. It would come as no surprise if the bags were suddenly to begin moving rhythmically, all of them together, displaying in a gaily-coloured, orgiastic dance all the seductiveness of which they were capable.

The guild feeling of these objects, their being together in their separation from everything different, is re-created by the passer-by according to his mood on each stroll through the souks. 'Today I'd like to explore the spices,' he says to himself, and the wonderful blend of smells is already in his nostrils and the great baskets of red peppers before his eyes. 'Today I feel like some dyed wools,' and there they hang, crimson, deep blue, bright yellow, and black, all around him. 'Today I want to see the baskets and watch them being woven.'

It is astounding what dignity they achieve, these things that men have made. They are not always beautiful; more and more trash of dubious origin finds its way in here, machine-made imports from the northern countries. But they still present themselves in the old way. In addition to the booths that are only for selling there are many where you can stand and watch the things being manufactured. You are in on the process from the start, and seeing it makes you feel good. Because part of the desolation of our modern life is the fact that we get everything delivered to the door ready for consumption as if it came out of some horrid conjuring device. But here you can see the rope-maker busy at his work, and his stock of finished ropes hangs beside him. In tiny booths hordes of small boys, six or seven of them at a time, operate lathes while youths assemble the pieces the boys have turned for them into little low tables. The wool with its wonderful, glowing colours is dyed before your eyes, and there are boys sitting about everywhere knitting caps in gay, attractive patterns.

Their activity is public, *displaying* itself in the same

way as the finished goods. In a society that conceals so much, that keeps the interior of its houses, the figures and faces of its women, and even its places of worship jealously hidden from foreigners, this greater openness with regard to what is manufactured and sold is doubly seductive.

What I really wanted to do was to find out how bargaining worked, but whenever I entered the souks I temporarily lost sight of the bargaining for the things that were its object. To the naive observer there seems to be no reason why a person should turn to one morocco merchant in particular when there are twenty others beside him whose wares hardly differ from his own. You can go from one to another and back again to the first. Which stall you will buy from is never certain in advance. Even if, say, you have made up your mind to this or that, you have every opportunity of changing it.

Nothing, neither doors nor windows, separates the passer-by from the merchandise. The merchant, sitting among the latter, has no name on display and is able, as I have said, to reach everything with ease. The passer-by finds each object obligingly held out to him. He may hold it in his hand for a long time, discuss it thoroughly, ask questions, express doubts, and, if he likes, tell his life story or the history of his tribe or the history of the whole world without making a purchase. The man among his wares has one quality above all else: he is composed. There he sits. He has little room or opportunity for expansive gestures. He belongs to his wares as much as they to him. They are not packed away somewhere; he always has his hands or his eyes on them. There is an intimacy, an alluring intimacy between him and his things. He watches over them and keeps them in order as if they were his enormous family.

It neither bothers nor embarrasses him that he knows their precise value, because he keeps it a secret and you will never discover it. This lends a touch of heady mystery to the bargaining process. Only he can tell how close you come to his secret, and he is an expert at vigorously parrying every thrust so that the protective distance to that value is never threatened. It is considered honourable in the purchaser not to let himself be cheated, but this is no easy undertaking for him because he is always groping in the dark. In countries where the price ethic prevails, where fixed prices are the rule, there is nothing to going shopping. Any fool can go out and find what he needs. Any fool who can read figures can contrive not to get swindled.

In the souks, however, the price that is named first is an unfathomable riddle. No one knows in advance what it will be, not even the merchant, because in any case there are many prices. Each one relates to a different situation, a different customer, a different time of day, a different day of the week. There are prices for single objects and prices for two or more together. There are prices for foreigners visiting the city for a day and prices for foreigners who have been here for three weeks. There are prices for the poor and prices for the rich, those for the poor of course being the highest. One is tempted to think that there are more kinds of prices than there are kinds of people in the world.

Yet that is only the beginning of a complicated affair regarding the outcome of which nothing is known in advance. It is said that you should get down to about a third of the original price, but this is nothing but a rough estimate and one of those vapid generalizations with which people are brushed off who are either unwilling or unable to go into the finer points of this age-old ritual.

It is desirable that the toing and froing of negotiations should last a miniature, incident-packed eternity. The merchant is delighted at the time you take over your purchase. Arguments aimed at making the other give ground should be far-fetched, involved, emphatic, and stimulating. You can be dignified or eloquent, but you will do best to be both. Dignity is employed by both parties to show that they do not attach too much importance to either sale or purchase. Eloquence serves to soften the opponent's resolution. Some arguments merely arouse scorn; others cut to the quick. You must try everything before you surrender. But even when the time has come to surrender it must happen suddenly and unexpectedly so that your opponent is thrown into confusion and for a moment lets you see into his heart. Some disarm you with arrogance, others with charm. Every trick is admissible, any slackening of attention inconceivable.

In the booths that are large enough to walk around in the vendor very often takes a second opinion before yielding. The man he consults, a kind of spiritual head as regards prices, stands in the background and takes no part in the proceedings; he is there, but he does not bargain himself. He is simply turned to for final decisions. He is able, as it were against the vendor's will, to sanction fantastic deviations in the price. But because it is done by *him*, who has not been involved in the bargaining, no one has lost face.

The cries of the blind

Here I am, trying to give an account of something, and as soon as I pause I realize that I have not yet said anything at all. A marvellously luminous, viscid substance is left behind in me, defying words. Is it the language I did not understand there, and that must now gradually find its translation in me? There were incidents, images, sounds, the meaning of which is only now emerging; that words neither recorded nor edited; that are beyond words, deeper and more equivocal than words.

A dream: a man who unlearns the world's languages until nowhere on earth does he understand what people are saying.

What is there in language? What does it conceal? What does it rob one of? During the weeks I spent in Morocco I made no attempt to acquire either Arabic or any of the Berber languages. I wanted to lose none of the force of those foreign-sounding cries. I wanted sounds to affect me as much as lay in their power, unmitigated by deficient and artificial knowledge on my part. I had not read a thing about the country. Its customs were as unknown to me as its people. The little that one picks up in the course of one's life about every country and every people fell away in the first few hours.

But the word 'Allah' remained; there was no getting round that. With it I was equipped for that part of my experience that was most ubiquitous and insistent, and most persistent: the blind. Travelling, one accepts everything; indignation stays at home. One looks, one listens,

one is roused to enthusiasm by the most dreadful things
✓ because they are new. Good travellers are heartless.

Last year, approaching Vienna after a fifteen-year ab-
sence, I passed through *Blindenmarkt* – in English 'Blind
Market', as one might say 'Slave Market' – a place whose
existence I had never previously suspected. The name
struck me like a whiplash, and it has stayed with me since.
This year, arriving in Marrakesh, I suddenly found myself
among the blind. There were hundreds of them, more than
one could count, most of them beggars. A group of them,
sometimes eight, sometimes ten, stood close together in
a row in the market, and their hoarse, endlessly repeated
chant was audible a long way off. I stood in front of them,
as still as they were, and was never quite sure whether they
sensed my presence. Each man held out a wooden alms
dish, and when someone tossed something in the proffered
coin passed from hand to hand, each man feeling it, each
man testing it, before one of them, whose office it was,
finally put it into a pouch. They *felt* together, just as
they murmured and called together.

All the blind offer one the name of God, and by giving
alms one can acquire a claim on him. They begin with God,
they end with God, they repeat God's name ten thousand
times a day. All their cries contain a declension of his
name, but the call they have once settled on always remains
the same. The calls are acoustical arabesques around God,
but how much more impressive than optical ones. Some
rely on his name alone and cry nothing else. There is a
terrible defiance in this; God seemed to me like a wall
that they were always storming in the same place. I believe
those beggars keep themselves alive more by their formulas
than by the yield of their begging.

Repetition of the same cry characterizes the crier. You commit him to memory, you know him, from now on he is there; and he is there in a sharply defined capacity: in his cry. You will learn no more from him; he shields himself, his cry being also his border. In this one place he is precisely what he cries, no more, no less: a beggar, blind. But the cry is also a multiplication; the rapid, regular repetition makes of him a group. There is a peculiar energy of asking in it; he is asking on behalf of many and collecting for them all. 'Consider all beggars! Consider all beggars! God will bless you for every beggar you give to.'

It is said that the poor will enter paradise five hundred years before the rich. By giving alms you buy a bit of paradise from the poor. When someone has died you 'follow on foot, with or without trilling mourners, swiftly to the grave, in order that the dead shall soon achieve bliss. *Blind men sing the creed.'*

Back from Morocco, I once sat down with eyes closed and legs crossed in a corner of my room and tried to say 'Alláh! Alláh! Alláh!' over and over again for half an hour at the right speed and volume. I tried to imagine myself going on saying it for a whole day and a large part of the night; taking a short sleep and then beginning again; doing the same thing for days and weeks, months and years; growing old and older and living like that, and clinging tenaciously to that life; flying into a fury if something disturbed me in that life; wanting nothing else, sticking to it utterly.

I understood the seduction there is in a life that reduces everything to the simplest kind of repetition. How much or how little variety was there in the activities of the craftsmen I had watched at work in their little booths? In the

haggling of the merchant? In the steps of the dancer?
In the countless cups of peppermint tea that all the visitors
here take? How much variety is there in money? How
much in hunger?

I understood what those blind beggars really are: the
saints of repetition. Most of what for us still eludes repetition is eradicated from their lives. There is the spot where
they squat or stand. There is the unchanging cry. There
is the limited number of coins they can hope for. Three or
four different denominations. There are the givers, of
course, who are different, but blind men do not see them,
and their way of expressing their thanks makes sure that
the givers too are all made the same.

The marabout's saliva

I had turned away from the group of eight blind beggars,
their litany still in my ear, and gone only a few steps
farther when my attention was caught by a white-haired
old man standing quite alone with his legs slightly apart;
he held his head a little on one side and he was chewing.
He too was blind and, to judge from the rags he was
dressed in, a beggar. But his cheeks were full and red,
his lips healthy and moist. He was chewing slowly with
his mouth closed and the expression on his face was a
cheerful one. He chewed thoroughly, as if following in-
structions. It evidently gave him much pleasure, and
watching him I was put in mind of his saliva and the
fact that he must have a great deal of it. He was standing
in front of a row of stalls on which mountains of oranges

were banked up for sale; I said to myself that one of the
stall-keepers must have given him an orange and that he
was chewing that. His right hand stood a little way away
from his body. The fingers of that hand were all widely
splayed. It looked as if they were paralysed and he could
not close them.

There was quite a lot of free space around the old man,
which in this busy spot I found surprising. He gave the
impression that he was always alone and did not wish it
otherwise. I resolutely watched him chewing, intending to
wait and see what happened when he had finished. It took
a very long time; I had never seen a man chew so heartily
and so exhaustively. I felt my own mouth begin to move
slightly although it contained nothing that it could have
chewed. I experienced something akin to awe at his enjoyment, which struck me as being more conspicuous than
anything I had ever seen in association with a human
mouth. His blindness failed to fill me with compassion.
He seemed collected and content. Not *once* did he interrupt
himself to ask for alms as the others all did. Perhaps he
had what he wanted. Perhaps he did not need anything
else.

When he had finished he licked his lips a few times;
stretched his right hand with the splayed fingers a little
farther forward, and in a hoarse voice said his piece. I
went up to him rather shyly and laid a coin on his palm.
The fingers remained stretched; he really could not close
them. Slowly he raised the hand towards his face. He
pressed the coin to his protruding lips and took it into
his mouth. Hardly was it inside before he began chewing
again. He pushed the coin this way and that in his mouth
and it seemed to me I could follow its movements : now it

was on the left, now on the right, and he was chewing as exhaustively as before.

I was amazed and I was dubious. I wondered whether I was not mistaken. Perhaps the coin had meanwhile disappeared somewhere else and I had not noticed. I waited again. When he had chewed with the same enjoyment and was finished, the coin appeared between his lips. He spat it into his left hand, which he had raised. A great deal of saliva streamed out with it. Then he slipped the coin into a pouch that he wore on his left.

I tried to dissolve my disgust at this proceeding in its outlandishness. What could be filthier than money? But this old man was not I; what caused me disgust gave him enjoyment, and had I not sometimes seen people kissing coins? The copious saliva undoubtedly had a role to play here, and he was clearly distinguished from other beggars by his ample generation of saliva. He had put in long practice before ever asking for alms; whatever he had eaten before, no one else would have taken so long over it. There was some kind of meaning in the motions of his mouth.

Or had he only taken *my* coin in his mouth? Had he felt in the palm of his hand that it was of a higher denomination than he was usually given and wanted to express his special thanks? I waited to see what would happen next, and I did not find waiting difficult. I was bewildered and intrigued and would certainly not have been able to give my attention to anything but the old man. He repeated his formula a few times. An Arab came past and laid a much smaller coin on his palm. He lifted it to his mouth without hesitating, put it in, and began chewing exactly as before. Possibly he did not chew quite as long this time.

He spat the coin out, again with a great deal of saliva, and slipped it into his pouch. He was given other coins, some of them quite small, and the same proceeding was repeated several times. I became more and more perplexed; the longer I looked on, the less I understood why he did it. But one thing there was no doubting any more: he always did it, it was his habit, his particular way of begging, and the people who gave him something expected this expression of interest on the part of his mouth, which seemed to me redder every time he opened it.

I did not notice that people were also looking at me, and I must have presented a ridiculous spectacle. Possibly, who knows, I was even gaping open-mouthed. Then suddenly a man came out from behind his oranges, took a few steps towards me, and said soothingly: 'That's a marabout.' I knew that marabouts were holy men and that special powers were attributed to them. The word aroused awe in me and I felt my disgust immediately dwindle. I asked diffidently: 'But why does he put the coins in his mouth?' 'He always does that,' said the man, as if it had been the most natural thing in the world. He turned away from me and resumed his post behind his oranges. Only now did I notice that behind every stall there were two or three pairs of eyes trained on me. The astonishing creature was myself, who stood so long uncomprehending.

With this information I felt I had been dismissed and stayed no longer. The marabout is a holy man, I told myself, and everything about this holy man is holy, even his saliva. In bringing the givers' coins in contact with his saliva he confers a special blessing on them and thus enhances the merit they have acquired in heaven through their almsgiving. He was sure of paradise, and himself had something to give away that men needed much more than he needed their coins. Now I understood the cheerfulness that was in his blind face and that distinguished him from the other beggars I had seen hitherto.

I went away, but with him so much in mind that I talked about him to all my friends. None of them had ever noticed him and I sensed that they doubted the truth of my words. The next day I went back to the same spot but he was not there. I looked everywhere; he was not to be found. I looked every day; he did not come again. Perhaps he lived alone somewhere in the mountains and only rarely came to the city. I could have asked the orange vendors about him but I was ashamed to face them. He did not mean the same to them as he did to me, and whereas I was not in the least averse to talking about him to friends who had never seen him I tried to keep him separate from people who knew him well and to whom he was a familiar and natural figure. He knew nothing of me and they might perhaps have talked to him about me.

I saw him once more, exactly a week later, again on a Saturday evening. He was standing in front of the same stall, but he had nothing in his mouth and was not chewing. He said his piece. I gave him a coin and waited to see what would happen to it. He was soon chewing it assiduously again, but while he was still busy doing so a man came up to me and said his nonsense: 'That's a marabout. He's blind. He puts the coin in his mouth to feel how much you've given him.' Then he said something to the marabout in Arabic and pointed to me. The old man, his chewing finished, had spat the coin out again. He turned to me, his face shining. He said a blessing for me, which he repeated six times. The friendliness and warmth that passed across to me as he spoke were such as I had never had a person bestow on me before.

The silent house and the empty rooftops

In order to feel at home in a strange city you need to have a secluded room to which you have a certain title and in which you can be alone when the tumult of new and incomprehensible voices becomes too great. The room should be quiet; no one should see you make your escape there, no one see you leave. The best thing is when you can slip into a cul-de-sac, stop at a door to which you have the key in your pocket, and unlock it without a soul hearing.

You step into the coolness of the house and close the door behind you. It is dark, and for a moment you can see nothing. You are like one of the blind men in the squares and passages you have just left. But you very soon have your eyesight back. You see a stone stairway leading to the first floor, and at the top you find a cat. The cat embodies the noiselessness you have been longing for. You are grateful to it for being alive : a quiet life is possible, then. It is fed without crying 'Allah' a thousand times a day. It is not mutilated, nor is it obliged to bow to a terrible fate. Cruel it may be, but it does not say so.

You walk up and down and breathe in the silence. What has become of the atrocious bustle? The harsh light and the harsh sounds? The hundreds upon hundreds of faces? Few windows in these houses look onto the street, sometimes none at all; everything opens onto the court-

yard, and this lies open to the sky. Only through the courtyard do you retain a mellow, tempered link with the world
around you.

But you can also go up on the roof and see all the flat
roofs of the city at once. The impression is one of level-
ness, of everything being built in a series of broad terraces. You feel you could walk all over the city up there.
The narrow streets present no obstacle; you cannot see
them, you forget that there are streets. The Atlas gleam
close and you would take them for the Alps were the light
on them not brighter and were there not so many palm
trees between them and the city.

The minarets that rise here and there are not like church
spires. They are slender, but they do not taper; they are
the same width top and bottom, and what matters is the
platform in the sky from which the faithful are called to
prayer. A minaret is more like a lighthouse, but with a
voice for a light.

The space above the rooftops is peopled with swallows.
It is like a second city, except that here things happen as
fast as they happen slowly in the human streets below.
They never rest, those swallows, you wonder if they ever
sleep; idleness, moderation, and dignity are qualities they
lack. They snatch their prey in flight; maybe the roofs in
their emptiness look like a conquered land to them.

You see, you do not show yourself on the roof. Up
there, I had thought, I shall feast my eyes on the women
of fable; from there I shall overlook the neighbours'
courtyards and overhear their goings-on. The first time I
went up on the roof of my friend's house I was full of
expectations, and as long as I continued to gaze into the
distance, at the mountains and out over the city, he was

content and I could sense his pride at being able to show me something so beautiful. But he started to fidget when, tiring of the far off, I became curious as to the near at hand. He caught me glancing down into the courtyard of the house next door, where to my delight I had become aware of women's voices speaking Spanish.

'That's not done here,' he said. 'You mustn't do that. I've often been warned against it. It's considered indelicate to take any notice of what goes on next door. It's considered bad manners. In fact one oughtn't to show oneself on the roof at all, and a man certainly not. Sometimes the womenfolk go up on the roofs, and they want to feel undisturbed.'

'But there aren't any women up here at all.'

'We may have been seen,' said my friend. 'One gets a bad name. One doesn't address a veiled woman on the street, either.'

'What if I want to ask the way?'

'You must wait till a man comes along.'

'But surely you can sit up on your own roof, can't you? If you see someone on the next roof it's not your fault.'

'Then I must look away. I must show how uninterested I am. A woman's just come up on the roof behind us, an old servant. She has no idea I've seen her, but she's already going down again.'

She was gone before I could turn round.

'But then one's less free on the roof than one is on the street,' I protested.

'Certainly,' he said. 'One wants to avoid getting a bad name with one's neighbours.'

I watched the swallows and envied the way they went swooping at their ease over three, five, ten roofs at a time.

The woman at the grille

I was passing a small public fountain at which a youth was drinking. I turned off to the left and heard a soft, tender, caressing voice coming from above me. I looked up at a house opposite and saw, at first-floor level, behind a woven grille, the face of a young woman. She was unveiled and dark and held her face right up to the grille. She was pouring out a gentle stream of phrases, and all those phrases consisted of endearments. I was puzzled that she wore no veil. Her head was tilted slightly, and I sensed that she was speaking to me. Her voice never rose but remained uniformly soft, and with so caressing a quality in it that she might have been holding my head in her arms. But I could see no hands, she showed no more than her face; perhaps her hands were secured somewhere. The room she stood in was dark; in the street, where I was standing, the sun shone harshly. It was as if her words issued from a fountain, flowing into one another. I had never heard endearments in that language, but I sensed that that was what they were.

I wanted to go over and look at the door of the house the voice came from, but I was half afraid that a movement on my part might frighten the voice away like a bird, and what would I do if it fell silent? I tried to be as gentle and soft as the voice itself; I have never stepped so warily. And I managed not to frighten it. I could still hear the voice when I was right up to the house and could no longer see the face at the grille. The narrow building gave the impression of a ruined tower. There was a hole in the wall where the stones had fallen out. The completely plain door, consisting of a few wretched planks, was fastened with wire and looked as if it were not often opened. It was not an inviting house : you could not get in, and inside it was dark and very likely dilapidated. Just around the corner was a cul-de-sac, but it was deserted and silent there and I could see no one I might have asked. Even in the cul-de-sac I could still hear the fountain of the caressing voice; round the corner it was like a far-off murmuring. I went back, again took up a position at some distance from the house, looked up, and there was the oval face pressed to the grille and the lips moving to the tender words.

It seemed to me that they now had a slightly different quality; a vague pleading was audible in them, as if she had been saying: don't go away. Perhaps she had thought I had gone for good when I disappeared to examine house and door. Now I was back and I was to stay. How can I describe the effect that an unveiled female face, looking down from the height of a window, has on one in this city, in these narrow streets? There are few windows on the street and never anyone looking out of them. The houses are like walls; often you have the feeling of walking for a long time between walls, although you know they are houses : you can see the doors and the sparse, unused windows. It is like that with the women. They are shape-less sacks walking down the street; you can make out nothing, guess at nothing, and soon grow weary of the effort of trying to arrive at a firm idea of them. You dis-pense with women. But you do so reluctantly, and a woman who then appears at a window and even speaks to you and inclines her head slightly and does not go away, as if she had always been there waiting for you, and who then goes on speaking to you when you turn your back on her and steal away, who would so speak whether you were there or not, and always to you, always to everyone – such a woman is a prodigy, a vision, and you are inclined to regard her as more important than anything else that this city might have to offer.

I would have stood there much longer, only it was not an entirely unfrequented quarter. Veiled women coming up the street towards me took no exception whatever to their compeer at the grille. They passed the tower-like house as if no one had been speaking. They neither stopped nor looked up. Never changing their pace they approached the house and turned, right under the speaker's window, into the street where I was standing. I did sense, though, that they gave me disapproving looks. What was I doing there? Why was I standing there? What was I staring up at?

A group of schoolchildren came past. They were playing and joking as they went past and behaved as if they did not hear the sounds coming from above. They examined me: I was a less familiar figure to them than the unveiled woman. I was slightly ashamed of my standing there and staring. I sensed, however, that I would disappoint the face at the grille by going away; those words flowed on like a little river of bird sound. But now between them came the shrill cries of the children, who were slow in going. They had their satchels with them and were on the way home from school; they were trying to draw out the journey by inventing little games, one of the rules of which entailed their running forwards a little way, and then backwards. As a result they progressed at a snail's pace and made listening an ordeal to me.

A woman with a very small child halted beside me. She
must have come up from behind; I had not noticed her.
She did not stay long; she gave me a venomous look;
behind the veil I made out the features of an old woman.
She grasped the child as if my presence constituted a threat
to it and shuffled on without a word to me. Feeling uncomfortable, I left my post and slowly followed her. She
went a few houses farther down the street and then turned
off. When I reached the corner round which she had
disappeared I saw, at the bottom of a cul-de-sac, the dome
of a small koubba. A koubba is a shrine in which a saint
is buried and to which people make pilgrimages with their
wishes. The old woman stopped in front of the closed
door of the koubba and lifted the tiny child up, pressing
its mouth to a object that I could not make out from where
I was standing. She repeated this movement several times,
then set the child down, took its hand, and turned to go.
At the end of the cul-de-sac she had to pass me again,
but this time she did not even give me a venomous look
before going off in the direction we had both come from.

I went up to the koubba myself and saw, halfway up the
wooden door, a ring wound round with old rags. It was
these the child had kissed. The whole episode had taken
place in complete silence, and in my embarrassment I had
failed to notice that the schoolchildren were standing behind me and watching me. Suddenly I heard their ringing
laughter as three or four of them made a rush for the door,
seized the ring, and kissed the old rags. Laughing loudly,
they repeated this ritual from all sides. One hung from the
right side of the ring, another from the left, and their
kisses were like a series of loud smacks. Soon they were
shoved aside by others behind them. They all wanted to

show me how it should be done; perhaps they expected me to imitate them. They were clean children, all of them, and well looked-after; I was sure they were washed several times a day. But the rags looked as dirty as if the alley had been wiped with them. They were supposed to be shreds of the saint's own robe and for the faithful there was something of his holiness in them.

When the boys had had their fill of kissing them they came after me and milled around me. One of them attracted my attention by his intelligent face and I saw he would have liked to speak to me. I asked him in French whether he could read. He answered with a well-mannered 'oui, monsieur'. I took a book from under my arm, opened it, and held it out to him; slowly but faultlessly he read the French sentences aloud. It was a work on the religious customs of the Moroccans, and the passage I had opened it at dealt with the veneration of the saints and their koubbas. You can call it an accident if you like, but he now read out to me what he and his friends had just demonstrated to me. Not that he gave any indication of being aware of this; perhaps in the excitement of reading he did not take in the meaning of the words. I praised him, and he accepted my tribute with the dignity of an adult. I liked him so much that I involuntarily associated him with the woman at the grille.

I pointed in the direction of the half-ruined house and asked: 'That woman at the grille up there – do you know her?'

'Oui, monsieur,' he said, and his face became very serious.

'Elle est malade?' I went on.

'Elle est très malade, monsieur.'

The 'very' that reinforced my question rang like a complaint, but a complaint about something to which he was wholly resigned. He was perhaps nine years old, but he looked then as if he had been living for twenty years with a chronic invalid, well knowing how a person ought to conduct himself in such a case.

'Elle est malade dans sa tête, n'est-ce pas?'

'Oui, monsieur, dans sa tête.' He nodded as he said 'in the head', but instead of pointing to his own head he pointed to that of another boy, who was exceptionally beautiful: he had a long, pale face with large, dark, very sad eyes. None of the children laughed. They stood there in silence. Their mood had changed: the moment I had started talking about the woman at the grille.

A visit to the Mellah

On the third morning, as soon as I was alone, I found my way to the Mellah. I came to a cross-roads where there were a great many Jews standing about. The traffic streamed past them and round a corner. I saw people going through an arch that looked as if it had been let into a wall, and I followed them. Inside the wall, enclosed by it on all four sides, lay the Mellah, the Jewish quarter.

I found myself in a small, open bazaar. Men squatted among their wares in little low booths; others, dressed European style, sat or stood. The majority had on their heads the black skull-cap with which the Jews here mark themselves out, and a great many wore beards. The first shops I came to sold material. One man was measuring

off silk. Another bent thoughtfully over his swiftly-
moving pencil, reckoning. Even the more richly-appointed
shops seemed very small. Many had callers; in one of the
booths two very fat men were carelessly ensconced about
a third, lean man – the proprietor – and were holding a
lively yet dignified discussion with him.

I walked past as slowly as possible and looked at the
faces. Their heterogeneity was astonishing. There were
faces that in other clothing I would have taken for Arab.
There were luminous old Rembrandt Jews. There were
Catholic priests of wily quietness and humility. There were
Wandering Jews whose restlessness was written in every
lineament. There were Frenchmen. There were Spaniards.
There were ruddy-complexioned Russians. There was one
you felt like hailing as the patriarch. Abraham; he was
haughtily addressing Napoleon, and a hot-tempered know-
all who looked like Goebbels was trying to butt in. I
thought of the transmigration of souls. Perhaps, I wondered, every human soul has to be a Jew once, and here
they all are: none remembers what he was before, and
even when this is so clearly revealed in his features that I,
a foreigner, can recognize it, every one of these people
still firmly believes he stands in direct line of descent
from the people of the Bible.

But there was something that they all had in common,
and as soon as I had accustomed myself to the rich variety
of their faces and their expressions I tried to find out what
it was. They had a way of swiftly glancing up and forming
an opinion of the person going past. Not *once* did I pass
unnoticed. When I stopped they would scent a purchaser
and examine me accordingly. But mostly I caught the
swift, intelligent look long before I stopped, and I even

caught it when I was walking on the other side of the street. Even in the case of the few who lay there with Arab indolence, the look was never indolent: it came, a practised scout, and swiftly moved on. There were hostile looks among them; cold, indifferent, disapproving, and infinitely wise looks. But none of them struck me as stupid. They were the looks of people who are always on their guard but who, expecting hostility, do not wish to evoke it: no trace of a challenge; and a fear that is careful to keep itself hidden.

One is almost inclined to say that the dignity of these people lies in their circumspection. The shop is open on one side only and they have no need to worry about anything going on behind their backs. In the street, the same people feel less secure. I soon noticed that the 'Wandering Jews' among them, the ones who gave a restless, dubious impression, were always *passers-by*; people who carried all their wares with them and were obliged to force their way through the crowd; who never knew whether someone was not about to pounce on their wretched stock from behind, from the left, from the right, or from all sides at once. The man who had a shop of his own and spent his day in it had a quality almost of assurance.

Some, however, squatted in the street and offered bits and pieces for sale. Often these were miserable little heaps of vegetables or fruit. It was as if the vendors actually had nothing at all to sell but were merely clinging to the gestures of commerce. They looked neglected; there were a great many of them, and I did not find it easy to get used to them. Before long, though, I was prepared for anything, and it caused me no particular surprise to see an aged and infirm man squatting on the ground and offering for sale a single, shrivelled lemon.

I was now in a street that led from the bazaar at the entrance deeper into the Mellah. It was thronged with people. Among the innumerable men I noticed one or two women who went unveiled. An ancient, withered crone came shambling along, looking like the oldest thing on earth. Her eyes stared fixedly into the distance as if she saw exactly where she was going. She stepped aside for no one; where others described curves to get through, she always had room around her. I believe people were afraid of her: she walked very slowly and would have had time to throw a curse on every living creature. It was probably the fear she inspired that gave her the strength for this walk. When at last she had gone by me I turned to look after her. She felt my eyes on her, because she slowly swivelled round, as slowly as she walked, and turned her gaze full on me. I hurried on; and so instinctive had been my reaction to her look that it was not for some time that I noticed how much faster I was now walking.

I passed a row of barber shops. Young men, the hair-dressers, lounged outside. On the ground opposite a man offered a basket of roast locusts for sale. I thought of the famous plague of Egypt and was surprised that Jews too ate locusts. Squatting in a booth that lay higher than the others was a man with the features and colouring of a Negro. He wore the Jewish skull-cap, and he was selling coal. The coal was stacked up high all around him; he looked as if he was to be walled in with coal and was just waiting for the men to come along and complete the job. He sat so still that at first I did not see him; it was his eyes that caught my attention, shining in the middle of all that coal. Next to him a one-eyed man was selling vegetables. The eye he could not see with was atrociously swollen; it was like a threat. He was fiddling confusedly with his vegetables. He pushed them gingerly across to one side, then pushed them gingerly back again. Another man squatted beside five or six stones lying on the ground. He picked one up, weighed it in his hand, inspected it, and held it up in the air for a moment. Then he put it back with the others, repeating the same ritual with these. He did not *once* look up at me, although I had stopped right in front of him. He was the only person in the entire quarter who disdained to look at me. The stones he was trying to sell took up his whole attention; he seemed to be more interested in them than in purchasers.

I noticed how, the deeper I penetrated into the Mellah, the poorer everything became. The beautiful woollens and silks were behind me. No one looked wealthy and princely like Abraham. The bazaar by the entrance gate had been a kind of posh quarter; the actual life of the Mellah, the life of the simple people, went on here. I came into a small square that struck me as being the heart of the Mellah. Men and women stood together around an oblong fountain. The women carried pitchers that they filled with water. The men were filling their leather water-containers. Their donkeys stood beside them, waiting to be watered. A few open-air cooks squatted in the middle of the square. Some were frying meat, others little doughnuts. They had their families with them, their wives and children; it was as if they had moved house out into the square and were living and cooking their meals here now.

Peasants in Berber costume stood around with live hens in their hands; they held them by the legs, which were tied together, their heads dangling down. When women approached they held the hens out to them to feel. The woman took the bird in her hand without the Berber's releasing it, without its altering its position. She pressed it and pinched it, her fingers going straight to the places where it ought to be meaty. No one said a word during this examination, neither the Berber nor the woman; the bird too remained silent. Then she left it in his hand, where it continued to dangle, and moved on to the next peasant. A woman never bought a hen without first examining a great many others.

The whole square was lined with shops; in some of them craftsmen were at work, their hammering and tapping sounding loud above the noise of voices. In one corner of the square a large number of men were gathered together in ardent debate. I did not understand what they were saying but to judge from their faces they were discussing the affairs of the world. They were of different opinions and they were fencing with arguments; it seemed to me that they laid into one another's arguments with gusto.

In the middle of the square stood an old beggar, the first I had seen here; he was not a Jew. With the coin he received he made immediately for one of the little doughnuts that were sizzling in the pan. There were a good many customers round the cook and the old beggar had to wait his turn. But he remained patient, even with his pressing desire on the threshold of fulfilment. When at last he had got his doughnut he took it back with him to the middle of the square and there ate it with mouth wide open. His relish spread like a cloud of contentment over the square. No one took any notice of him, but everyone absorbed the flavour of his contentment and he seemed to me to be extremely important for the life and well-being of the square – its eating monument.

But I do not think it was only him I had to thank for the happy enchantment of that square. I had the feeling that I was really somewhere else now, that I had reached the goal of my journey. I did not want to leave; I had been here hundreds of years ago but I had forgotten and now it was all coming back to me. I found exhibited the same density and warmth of life as I feel in myself. I *was* the square as I stood in it. I believe I am it always.

I found parting from it so difficult that every five or ten minutes I would come back. Wherever I went from then on, whatever else I explored in the Mellah, I kept breaking off to return to the little square and cross it in one direction or another in order to assure myself that it was still there.

I turned first into one of the quieter streets in which there were no shops, only dwelling-houses. Everywhere, on the walls, beside doors, some way up from the ground, large hands had been painted, each finger clearly outlined, mostly in blue: they were for warding off the evil eye. It was the sign I found used most commonly, and people painted it up for preference on the place where they lived. Through open doors I had glimpses of courtyards; they were cleaner than the streets. Peace flowed out of them over me. I would have loved to step inside but did not dare, seeing no one. I would not have known what to say if I had suddenly come across a woman in such a house. I was myself alarmed at the thought of perhaps alarming someone. The silence of the houses communicated itself as a kind of wariness. But it did not last long. A high, thin noise that sounded at first like crickets grew gradually louder until I thought of an aviary full of birds. 'What can it be? There's no aviary here with hundreds of birds! Children! A school!' Soon there was no doubt about it: the deafening hubbub came from a school.

Through an open gateway I could see into a large courtyard. Perhaps two hundred tiny little children sat crammed together on benches; others were running about or playing on the ground. Most of those on the benches had primers in their hands. In groups of three or four they rocked violently backwards and forwards, reciting in high-pitched voices: 'Aleph. Beth. Gimel.' The little black heads darted rhythmically to and fro; one of them was always the most zealous, his movements the most vehement; and in his mouth the sounds of the Hebrew alphabet rang out like a decalogue in the making.

I had stepped inside and was trying to unravel the tangle of activity. The smallest children were playing on the floor. Among them stood a teacher, very shabbily dressed; in his right hand he held a leather belt, for beating. He came up to me obsequiously. His long face was flat and expressionless, its lifeless rigidity in marked contrast to the liveliness of the children. He gave the impression that he would never be able to master them, that he was too badly paid. He was a young man, but *their* youth made him old. He spoke no French, and I expected nothing of him. It was enough for me that I could stand there in the middle of the deafening noise and look around a bit. But I had underestimated him. Beneath his rigor mortis there lurked something like ambition: he wanted to show me what his children could do.

He called a little boy over, held a page of the primer

up in front of him in such a way that I could see it too, and pointed to Hebraic syllables in quick succession. He switched from line to line, backwards and forwards across the page at random; I was not to think the boy had learned it by heart and was reciting blind, without reading. The little fellow's eyes flashed as he read out: 'La–lo–ma–nu–she–ti–ba–bu.' He did not make a single mistake and did not falter once. He was his teacher's pride, and he read faster and faster. When he had finished and the teacher had taken the primer away I patted him on the head and praised him – in French, but *that* he understood. He retired to his bench and made as if he could no longer see me, while the next boy took his turn. This one was much shyer and made mistakes; the teacher released him with a gentle spank and fetched out one or two more children. Throughout this proceeding the din continued unabated, and the Hebraic syllables fell like raindrops in the raging sea of the school.

Meanwhile other children came up to me and stared at me inquisitively, some cheeky, some shy, some flirtatious. The teacher, in his impenetrable wisdom, ruthlessly drove off the shy ones while letting the cheeky ones do as they liked. He was the poor and unhappy overlord of this part of the school; when the performance was over the meagre traces of satisfied pride disappeared from his face. I thanked him very politely and, to give him a lift, somewhat condescendingly, as if I were an important visitor. His satisfaction must have been obvious; with the clumsiness of touch that dogged me in the Mellah I determined to return next day and only then give him some money. I stayed a moment longer, watching the boys at their reciting. Their rocking to and fro appealed to me; I liked them best of all. Then I left, but the din I took with me. It accompanied me all the way to the end of the street.

This now started to become busier, as if it led to some important public place. Some way in front of me I could see a wall and a large gateway. I did not know where it led to, but the closer I got to it the more beggars I saw, sitting on either side of the street. I was puzzled by them, not having seen any Jewish beggars before. When I reached the gateway I saw ten or fifteen of them, men and women, mostly old people, squatting in a row. I stood rather self-consciously in the middle of the street and pretended to be examining the gate, whereas in reality I was studying the faces of the beggars.

A young man came over to me, pointed to the wall, said 'le cimetière israélite', and offered to take me in. They were the only words of French he spoke. I followed him quickly through the gate. He moved fast, and there was nothing to say. I found myself in a very bare, open space where not a blade of grass grew. The gravestones were so low that you hardly noticed them; you tripped over them as if they had been ordinary stones. The cemetery looked like a vast heap of rubble; perhaps that was what it had been once, only later being assigned its more serious purpose. Nothing in it stood up to any height. The stones you could see and the bones you could imagine were all *lying*. It was not a pleasant thing to walk erect; you could take no pride in doing so, you only felt ridiculous.

Cemeteries in other parts of the world are designed in such a way as to give joy to the living. They are full of things that are alive, plants and birds, and the visitor, the only person among so many dead, feels buoyed up and strengthened. His own condition strikes him as en-

viable. He reads people's names on the gravestones; he
has survived them all. Without admitting it to himself,
he has something of the feeling of having defeated each
one of them in single combat. He is sad too, of course,
that so many are no more, but at the same time this makes
him invincible. Where else can he feel that? On what
battlefield of the world is he the sole survivor? Amid the
supine he stands erect. But so do the trees and gravestones.
They are planted and set up there and surround him like a
kind of bequest that is there to please him.

But in that desolate cemetery of the Jews there is nothing.
It is truth itself, a lunar landscape of death. Looking at
it, you could not care less who lies where. You do not
stoop down, you make no attempt to puzzle it out. There
they all lie like rubble and you feel like scurrying over
them, quick as a jackal. It is a wilderness of dead in which
nothing grows any more, the last wilderness, the very last
wilderness of all.

When I had gone a little farther I heard shouts behind
me. I turned round and stopped. On the inside of the wall
too, on either side of the gate, stood beggars. They were
bearded old men, some of them on crutches, some blind.
I was taken aback; I had not noticed them before. My
guide having been in such a hurry, a good hundred paces
lay between them and me. I hesitated to cross that stretch
of wasteland again before I had penetrated farther. But
they did not hesitate. Three of them detached themselves
from the group by the wall and came hobbling over in a
tremendous hurry. The one in front was a broad-should-
ered, heavy man with a huge beard. He had only one leg
and hurled himself forward with mighty thrusts of his
crutches. He was soon far ahead of the others. The low

gravestones were no obstacle to him; his crutches always found the right spot on the ground and never skidded. Like some threatening animal he came hurtling at me. In his face as it drew rapidly closer there was nothing to arouse sympathy. Like his whole figure it expressed a single, violent demand: 'I'm alive! Give!'

I had an inexplicable feeling that he wanted to slay me with his bulk; it was uncanny. My guide, a light, slim person with the movements of a lizard, pulled me swiftly away before he reached me. He did not want me giving anything to these beggars and shouted something at them in Arabic. The big man on crutches tried to follow us, but when he saw that we were faster he gave up and came to a standstill. I could hear his angry cursing for some time, and the voices of the others who had fallen behind joined with his in a chorus of ill will.

Relieved to have escaped them, I was at the same time ashamed of having roused their expectations in vain. The one-legged old man's onslaught had been foiled not by the stones, with which he and his crutches were familiar, but by the quickness of my guide. And God knows, victory in so unequal a contest was nothing to be proud of. Wanting to find out something about our wretched enemy, I questioned the guide. He did not understand a word, and instead of an answer a half-witted smile spread over his face. 'Oui,' he said, over and over again; 'oui.' I had no idea where he was leading me. After the episode with the old man, however, the wilderness was no longer quite so desolate. He was its rightful occupant, keeper of the bare stones, the rubble, and the invisible bones.

But I had overstated his importance, for before long I came upon an entire population domiciled here. Beyond a small rise we turned into a hollow and were suddenly standing in front of a tiny house of prayer. Outside it, in a semicircle, perhaps fifty beggars had taken up residence, a jumble of men and women afflicted with every infirmity under the sun, an entire tribe almost, except that the aged predominated. They had installed themselves in colourful groups on the ground and they now, by degrees, not too hastily, moved into action. They began muttering benedictions and stretching out their arms. But they did not approach too close before I had visited the house of prayer.

I looked into a very small oblong room in which hundreds of candles were burning. They were stuck in little glass cylinders and swimming in oil. Most of them were ranged on tables of normal height and you looked down on them as if they had been a book you were reading. A smaller number hung from the ceiling in large vessels. On either side of the room stood a man who was obviously appointed to say prayers. A few coins lay on the table near them. I hesitated on the threshold because I had nothing to cover my head with. The guide took off his skull-cap and handed it to me. I put it on, not without a certain awkwardness because it was very dirty. The prayer leaders were beckoning me and I stepped inside among the candles. They did not take me for a Jew and I said no prayer. The guide pointed to the coins and I understood what was now expected of me. I did not stay for more than a moment. I was awed by this little room in the wilderness that was filled with candles, that consisted of nothing but candles. They radiated a quiet serenity, as if nothing was quite over as long as they still burned. Perhaps these frail flames were all that was left of the dead.

But outside you became closely and densely aware of the passionate life of the beggars.

I was back among them and now they really moved into action. They pressed round me from all sides as if I might miss precisely *their* infirmity and brought it to my attention in an elaborate and at the same time extremely vigorous kind of dance. They clutched my knees and kissed the flaps of my jacket. They seemed to be blessing every bit of my body. It was as if a throng of people had brought their mouths and eyes and noses, their arms and legs, their rags and crutches, everything they had, everything they consisted of, to bear upon *praying* to you. I was frightened, but I cannot deny that I was also deeply moved and that my fright was soon lost in this emotion. Never before had people come physically so close to me. I forgot their dirt, I did not care, I forgot about lice. I could feel the seduction of having oneself dismembered alive for others. That terrible weight of worship seems to justify the sacrifice, and how could it not work miracles?

But my guide took care that I did not remain in the beggars' hands. His claims were older, and nothing had yet been done to satisfy them. I did not have enough change for everyone. He drove off the unappeased with a lot of yelping and barking and pulled me away by the arm. When we had the house of prayer behind us he said 'oui' three times with his half-witted smile, although I had not asked him anything. It no longer seemed the same rubble heap as I retraced my steps. I knew now where its life and light were gathered. The old man inside the gate who had thrown himself with such vigour into the race on his crutches gave me a dark look; he said nothing, however, and kept his curse to himself. I passed out through the gate of the cemetery and my guide disappeared as swiftly as he had come, and at the same spot. It is possible he lived in a crack in the cemetery wall and emerged only rarely. He did not go without first having accepted his due, and by way of farewell he said 'oui'.

The Dahan family

Returning to the Mellah next day, I went as quickly as I could to the little square I called its 'heart' and then to the school, where I owed a debt to the teacher with the expressionless face. He received me exactly as before, just as if this had been my first visit, and possibly he would have gone through the whole performance with the reading again; I forestalled him, however, and gave him what I felt I owed him. He took the money quickly, without any hesitation and with a smile that made his face look even more stiff and stupid. I strolled among the children for a while, watching the rhythmic reading movements that had made such an impression on me the day before. Then, leaving the school, I began to wander at random through the streets of the Mellah. My desire to set foot inside one of the houses had increased. I had made up my mind not to leave the Mellah this time without having seen a house from inside. But how was I to get inside? I needed a pretext, and, as luck would have it, one soon presented itself.

I had stopped in front of one of the larger houses, the gateway of which was distinguished from the others by a certain respectability. The gate was open and I could see into a courtyard on the other side of which sat a woman. She was young, dark, and very radiant. Perhaps it had been she that had first attracted my attention. There were children playing in the courtyard, and having some experience with schools already I conceived the idea of pretending that I had taken the house for a school and was interested in the children.

I stood there and was staring inside over the children's heads at the woman, when presently a tall young man I had not noticed before detached himself from the background and came towards me. He was slim and held his head high, looking very noble in his flowing robe. He halted in front of me, gave me a look of stern scrutiny, and asked me in Arabic what I wanted. My response was to ask in French: 'Is this a school here?' He did not understand me, hesitated for a moment, said 'Attendez!', and left me. It was not the only word of French he spoke because when he returned with a younger person, who was spruced up in the French fashion in a European suit and as if he had been on holiday, he said 'mon frère' and also 'parle français'.

The younger brother had a flat, dull-looking peasant face and was very brown. In different clothing I would have taken him for a Berber, though not a handsome one. He really did speak French, and he asked me what I wanted. 'Is this a school?' I asked, feeling slightly guilty by this time because I had been unable to refrain from casting another glance at the woman in the courtyard beyond him, and this had not escaped him.

'No,' said the younger brother. 'There was a wedding here yesterday.'

'A wedding? Yesterday?' I was quite amazed, God

knows why, and my lively reaction evidently prompted him to add:

'My brother got married.'

With a nod he indicated the elder brother, the one I found so distinguished. I ought at this point to have thanked them for the information and gone on my way. But I hesitated, and the young husband said with a sweeping gesture of invitation: 'Entrez! Come in!' The brother added: 'Would you like to see the house?' Thanking them, I stepped into the courtyard.

The children – there were perhaps a dozen of them – scattered to make way, and I crossed the courtyard with the two brothers accompanying me. The radiant young woman rose to her feet – she was even younger than I had thought; sixteen, perhaps – and was introduced to me by the younger brother as his sister-in-law. It was she who had got married the day before. A door was opened to a room on the far side of the courtyard, and I was invited to enter. It was a smallish room, scrupulously tidy and clean, and it was furnished in European style: to the left of the door was a wide double bed, to the right of it a large, square table covered with a dark-green velvet cloth. A dresser, in which bottles and liqueur glasses were visible, stood against the wall beyond the table. The chairs around the table completed the picture, which could have been that of any modest petit-bourgeois home in France. Not a single object betrayed the country we were in. It was undoubtedly their best room; any other room in the house would have interested me more. But they thought to honour me by offering me a seat here.

The young woman, who understood French but hardly opened her mouth once, took a bottle and glasses from the dresser and poured me a glass of a powerful schnaps that the Jews distil here. It is called mahya, and they drink a great deal of it. In conversation with Moslems, who strictly speaking are not allowed to drink any alcohol at all, I often had the impression that they envied the Jews their mahya. The younger brother raised his glass to me and we drank. The three of us had sat down – he, his sister-in-law, and I – while the elder brother, the bridegroom, stood in the doorway for a few moments as a matter of courtesy and then went about his business. Probably he had a lot to do, and not being able to make himself understood to me in any case he left me to his wife and his brother.

The woman considered me with her motionless brown eyes; her gaze never left me, although not the faintest flicker of expression in her face showed what she thought of me. She wore a simple flowered dress that might have come from a French department store; it matched the room. Her young brother-in-law in his dark-blue, ridiculously well-ironed suit looked as if he had just stepped out of the window of a Paris outfitter's. The only foreign element in the whole room was their dark-brown skin.

All through the polite questions that the young man asked me and that I as politely if not quite as stiffly tried to answer, I was thinking that the beautiful, silent person sitting opposite me had shortly before risen from her bridal bed. The morning was already far advanced, but today she would undoubtedly have got up late. I was the first stranger she had seen since this crucial change in her life had occurred. My curiosity about her was as great as hers about me. It had been her eyes that had drawn me into the house, and now she was staring at me in steadfast silence as I chattered away, though not to her. I remember that during that session a quite absurd hope filled me. I hoped that she was mentally comparing me with her groom, whom I had liked so much; I made a wish that she would prefer him to me, his simple nobility and easy dignity to my presumptuous foreignness, behind which she may have imagined power or wealth. I wished him my defeat, and his marriage had my blessing.

The young man asked me where I came from.

'From England,' I said. 'London.' I had made a habit of giving this simplified version of the facts in order to avoid confusing people. I sensed a slight disappointment at my answer but did not know what he would have preferred to hear.

'You're visiting here, then?'

'Yes, I had never seen Morocco before.'

'Have you been in the Bahía yet?'

He proceded to question me about all the official sights of the city: had I been here or had I been there, in the end offering his services as guide. I knew that once you had put yourself in the hands of a native guide you saw nothing any more, and in order to kill this hope as swiftly as possible and turn the conversation to other topics I explained that I was here with an English film company that the Pasha had personally provided with a guide. Actually I had nothing to do with the film, but an English friend of mine, who was making it, had invited me to Morocco, and another friend who was with me, a young American, had a part in it.

My explanation had the desired effect. He no longer insisted on showing me the city: now quite different prospects opened up before his eyes. Did we perhaps have a job for him? He could do everything. He had been out

of work for a long time. His face, which had a sullen,
apathetic quality, had been a riddle to me up until now;
it rarely registered any reaction, or so slowly that you were
forced to conclude that there was nothing going on behind
it. Now I realized that his suit had misled me as to his
circumstances. Perhaps he took so gloomy a view of things
because he had been out of work for a long time, and
perhaps his family would not let him forget it. I knew
that all the minor posts in my friend's company had been
filled long ago and I told him so immediately lest there
should be any misunderstanding. Leaning closer to me
across the table he asked suddenly:

'Êtes-vous Israélite?'

I answered enthusiastically in the affirmative. It was such
a relief to be able to say 'yes' to something at last, and
besides I was curious as to what effect this admission would
have on him. He smiled all over his face and showed
his large, yellowish teeth. Turning to his sister-in-law,
who was sitting a little way off opposite me, he nodded
vigorously to communicate his delight at this news. She
did not turn a hair. She seemed if anything slightly disappointed; perhaps she would have liked the stranger to
be wholly foreign. He went on beaming, and as I began
asking questions myself he answered more fluently than
I would have expected him to do.

I discovered that his sister-in-law was from Mazagan.
The house was not always so full. The members of the
family had come from Casablanca and Mazagan to the
wedding and had brought their children. They were all
staying with them in the house and that was why the courtyard was so unusually crowded. He was called Élie Dahan
and was proud to learn that I had the same first name as

himself. His brother was a watchmaker, though without his own business; he worked for another watchmaker. I was repeatedly called upon to raise my glass, and a dish of preserved fruit was placed before me, the kind my mother used to make. My glass I raised but the fruit I politely refused – perhaps because it reminded me too much of home – thereby provoking a clear reaction on the sister-in-law's face: regret. I mentioned that my ancestors had come from Spain and asked whether there were still people in the Mellah who spoke old Spanish. He did not know of any, but he had heard about the history of the Jews in Spain, and this vague notion was the first thing that appeared to extend beyond his French get-up and the terms of his immediate environment. Now he started asking the questions again. How many Jews were there in England? How did they fare? How were they treated? Were there any great men among them? I suddenly felt something akin to a warm debt of gratitude to the country where I had fared well, where I had made friends, and in order that he should understand me I told him about an English Jew who had won high esteem in the field of politics, Lord Samuel.

'Samuel?' he asked, and the smile spread over his whole face once more so that I assumed he had heard of him and was familiar with his career. But I was wrong, because he turned to the young woman and said: 'That's my sister-in-law's name. Her father is called Samuel.' I gave her an inquiring look; she nodded vigorously.

From this moment on he became bolder in his questions. The feeling of being distantly related to Lord Samuel – a member, as I had told him, of British governments – spurred him on. Were there any other Jews in our com-

pany? One, I told him. Couldn't I bring him to see them?
I promised to do so. Were there no Americans with us?
It was the first time I had heard him say 'American'; I
sensed that it was a magic word with him and I knew now
why he had at first been disappointed to hear I came from
England. I told him about my American friend, who was
staying at the same hotel as ourselves; I had to admit,
though, that he was not 'Israélite'.

The elder brother came in again; perhaps he thought I
had been sitting there too long. He threw glances at his
wife. She was still staring at me. It occurred to me that
it was on her account I had stayed and that I had not given
up hope of getting into conversation with her. I suggested
to the younger brother that he call on me at my hotel if
he liked, and I stood up to go. I said goodbye to the young
woman. The two brothers saw me out. The bridegroom
stopped by the gate, rather as if he were barring my way,
and it struck me that he perhaps expected some remuner-
ation for having allowed me to view his house. On the
other hand I liked him as well as before and had no wish
to insult him, so that I stood there for a moment in a
state of the most acute embarrassment. My hand, which
had been approaching my pocket, stopped halfway, and
I caught it pretending to scratch. The younger brother
came to my rescue and said something in Arabic. I
heard the word 'Jehudi', Jew, relating to myself, and
was dismissed with a friendly, slightly disappointed
handshake.

Élie Dahan presented himself at my hotel the very next
day. I was not there, so he came back later. I was out a
great deal, and he had no luck; or perhaps he thought I
was there but refusing to receive him. The third or fourth

time he finally found me in. I invited him for coffee, and he came with me to the Djema el Fna, where we sat on one of the café terraces. He was dressed exactly as he had been the day before. At first he said little, but even his expressionless face made it clear that he had something on his mind. An old man approached our table selling chased brass salvers; from his black skull-cap, dress, and beard he was easily recognizable as a Jew. Élie bent mysteriously towards me and, as though he had something very special to confide to me, said: 'C'est un Israélite.' I nodded delightedly. Around us sat a lot of Arabs and one or two Europeans. Only now that the previous day's understanding between us had been re-established did he feel more at his ease and came out with his request.

Could I give him a letter to the commandant of Ben Guérir camp? He would like to work for the Americans.

'What sort of letter?' I asked.

'Tell the commandant to give me a job.'

'But I don't know the commandant.'

'Write him a letter,' he repeated, as if he had not heard me.

'I don't know the commandant,' I said again.

'Tell him to give me a job.'

'But I don't even know what his name is. How can I write to him if I don't know his name?'

'I'll tell you his name.'

'What sort of job do you want there?'

'Comme plongeur,' he said, and I vaguely remembered that that was someone who did the washing up.

'Were you there before?'

'I once worked for the Americans as "plongeur",' he said very proudly.

'At Ben Guérir?'

'Yes.'

'And why did you leave?'

'I was dismissed,' he said, just as proudly.

'Was that long ago?'

'A year.'

'Why don't you apply again?'

'People from Morocco aren't allowed in the camp. Only when they work there.'

'But why were you dismissed? Perhaps at the time you wanted to leave, did you?' I added tactfully.

'There wasn't enough work. They let a lot of people go.'

'Then there'll hardly be a job free for you if there's not enough work.'

'Write to the commandant to give me a job.'

'A letter from me would do no good at all because I don't know him.'

'With a letter they'll let me in.'

'But I'm not even an American. I told you – I'm English. Don't you remember?'

He frowned. It was the first time he had listened to an objection. He thought for a moment and then said: 'Your friend is an American.'

Now I had it. I, the real live friend of a real live American, was to write a letter to the commandant of Ben Guérir camp asking him to give Élie Dahan a job as 'plongeur'.

I said I would talk to my American friend. He would certainly know the right thing to do in the circumstances. Perhaps he would be able to write a letter himself, but of course I must ask him first. I knew for a fact that he was not personally acquainted with the commandant.

'Tell him in your letter to give my brother a job too.'

'Your brother? The watchmaker?'

'I have another brother – younger. He's called Simon.'

'What does he do?'

'He's a tailor. He worked for the Americans too.'

'As a tailor?'

'He counted laundry.'

'And he left them a year ago too?'

'No. He was dismissed a fortnight ago.'

'That means they no longer have a job for him.'

'Write for both of us. I'll give you the commandant's name. Write from your hotel.'

'I'll have a word with my friend.'

'Shall I pick up the letter at the hotel?'

'Come back in two or three days, when I've talked with my friend, and I'll tell you whether he can write a letter for you.'

'Do you not know the commandant's name?'

'No. You were going to tell me the name yourself, weren't you?'

'Shall I bring you the commandant's name to the hotel?'

'Yes. Do that.'

'I'll bring you the commandant's name today. You write him a letter telling him to give me and my brother a job.'

'Bring me the name tomorrow.' I was starting to become impatient. 'I can't promise anything before I've spoken to my friend.'

I cursed the moment when I had set foot in his family's house. Now he would come every day, possibly more than once, and repeat the same sentence over and over again.

I should never have accepted these people's hospitality.
At that very moment he said:

'Wouldn't you like to come back to our place?'

'Now? No, I haven't got time now. Some other time I'd
love to.'

I stood up and left the terrace. He stood up uncertainly
and followed me. I noticed he was hesitating, and when
we had gone a few paces he asked: 'Did you pay?'

'No.' I had forgotten. I had wanted to get away from
him as quickly as possible and forgotten to pay for the
coffee I had invited him to join me in. I was ashamed of
myself and my irritation evaporated. I went back, paid,
and strolled with him through the streets leading to the
Mellah.

He now fell into the role of guide, pointing out to me
all the things I knew already. His elucidations invariably
consisted of two sentences: 'That's the Bahía. Have you
been in the Bahía yet?' 'Those are the goldsmiths. Have
you seen the goldsmiths?' My replies were no less stereo-
typed: 'Yes, I've been inside' or 'Yes, I've seen them'. I
had one simple desire: to stop him taking me somewhere.
But he was determined to make himself useful to me, and
the determination of a stupid person is unshakable. When
I saw he was not going to let go I resorted to a ruse. I
asked about the Berrima, the Sultan's palace. That was
somewhere I had not been yet, I told him, well knowing
that you were not allowed inside.

'La Berrima?' he said delightedly. 'My aunt lives there.
Do you want me to take you?'

I could no longer say no. I failed to understand what
his aunt was doing in the Sultan's palace, though. Was
she a caretaker, perhaps? A washerwoman? A cook? I

rather fancied gaining entry to the palace in this way. Perhaps I could make friends with the aunt and learn something about the life there.

On the way to the Berrima our conversation turned to the Glaoui, the Pasha of Marrakesh. A few days before this someone had tried to assassinate the new Sultan of Morocco in the local mosque. Divine service was the only opportunity for the assassin to get physically close to the king. This new Sultan was an old man. He was the uncle of the one before, whom the French had deposed and banished from Morocco. Regarding the uncle-sultan as a tool of the French, the Freedom party opposed him with fair means and foul. Among native Moroccans he had only one powerful prop in the entire country, and that was El Glaoui, the Pasha of Marrakesh, who had been known for two generations as the most reliable ally the French had. The Glaoui had accompanied the new Sultan to the mosque and shot the assassin down where he stood. The Sultan himself had been only slightly wounded.

I and a friend had been out walking in that part of the city shortly before this happened. We had come across the mosque by chance and had stopped to watch the crowds that were waiting for the Sultan to arrive. The police were in a state of great excitement – there had already been a number of assassination attempts – and were going about their business clumsily and noisily. We too were waved on in an unfriendly manner, but the natives were shooed away with angry shouts when they stood in the very places they had been given permission to stand in. In the circumstances we felt little inclination to await the Sultan's arrival and continued on our way. Half an hour later the assassin struck, and the news spread like wildfire through

the city. Now here I was with this new companion, walking through the same streets as on that day – which was
what brought our talk round to the Glaoui.

'The Pasha hates the Arabs,' said Élie. 'He loves the
Jews. He is the Jews' friend. He does not let anything
happen to the Jews.'

He was talking more and faster than usual, and what he
said sounded very odd, as if he had learned it by heart
from an old history book. Not even the Mellah had struck
me with so medieval a quality as these words concerning
the Glaoui. I stole a glance at his face as he said them
again. 'The Arabs are his enemies. He has Jews around
him. He talks to Jews. He is the Jews' friend.' He preferred
the title 'Pasha' to the surname 'Glaoui'. Every time I
said 'Glaoui' he answered with 'Pasha'. He made it sound
like the word 'commandant', with which he had been
driving me mad shortly before. But his highest and
hopefullest word was, the Glaoui notwithstanding,
'American'.

Meanwhile we had passed through a little gate into a
quarter that lay outside the city wall. The houses consisted of a single storey and exuded an air of great poverty.
We hardly passed a soul in the narrow, uneven lanes –
only a few children playing here and there. I was wondering how we were going to get to the palace this way
when he stopped in front of one of the more inconspicuous-
looking houses and said:

'Here is my aunt.'

'Does she not live in the Berrima?'

'This is the Berrima,' he said. 'The whole quarter is
called Berrima.'

'And Jews can live here too?'

'Yes,' he said, 'the Pasha gave permission.'

'Are there many here?'

'No, most of the people here are Arabs. But some Jews live here too. Don't you want to meet my aunt? My grandmother lives here too.'

I was delighted to have another opportunity of seeing a house from inside, and I counted myself fortunate that it was so simple and unpretentious a house. I was pleased with the swap, and had I grasped it from the start I should have looked forward to it more than to a visit to the Sultan's palace.

He knocked and we waited. After a while a sturdy young woman with open, friendly features appeared. She led the way inside. She was a little embarrassed because all the rooms had just been painted and there was nowhere she could receive us in the proper manner. We stood in the small courtyard, off which there were three small rooms. Élie's grandmother was there. She did not seem old at all. She greeted us with a smile, but I had the impression that she was not particularly proud of him.

Three small children were yelling their lungs out. They were very small and wanted to be picked up; the two smallest were making an ear-splitting din. Élie was talking urgently to his young aunt. He had an astonishing amount to say. His Arabic took on a vehemence of which I would not have thought him capable, but perhaps it was due more to the nature of the language.

I liked the aunt. She was a well-developed young woman and she was looking at me in a wondering and far from servile way. She put me in mind at first glance of the kind of oriental women Delacroix painted. She had the same elongated and yet full face, the same eyes, the same straight,

slightly overlong nose. I was standing very close to her in
the tiny courtyard and our glances met in response to a
natural pull. I was so affected that I dropped my eyes, but
then I saw her strong ankles, which were as attractive as
her face. I would have liked to sit beside her. She said
nothing as Élie went on and on at her and the children
yelled louder and louder. Her mother was no farther from
me than she was herself. She's sure to sense something,
I thought, and I began to feel awkward. The scanty furni-
ture was piled high in the courtyard and the rooms into
which one could see were empty; there was nowhere we
could have sat down. The walls were freshly whitewashed
as if these people had just moved in. The young woman
smelled as clean as her walls. I tried to imagine her
husband, envying him. I bowed, shook hands with her
mother and her, and turned to go.

Élie came with me. Outside in the lane he said: 'She
is sorry that they are doing the cleaning.' I could not
contain myself and said: 'Your aunt is a lovely woman.'
I had to tell someone and possibly I also hoped against
all reason that he would reply: 'She wants to see you
again.' But he was silent.

So little notice did he take of my inexplicable fancy
that he suggested he now take me to see an uncle. I
accepted, slightly ashamed at having given myself away;
perhaps I had committed a breach of etiquette. An ugly or
boring uncle would offset the lovely aunt.

On the way he explained his intricate family relation-
ships. Actually they were more extensive than intricate;
he had relatives in a variety of towns in Morocco. I brought
the conversation round to the sister-in-law I had seen the
day before, asking about her father in Mazagan. 'C'est un

pauvre,' he said, 'a poor man.' He was the man, you will remember, who was called Samuel. He brought in nothing. His wife worked for him; she alone kept the family going. Were there many poor Jews in Marrakesh? I wanted to know. 'Two hundred and fifty,' he said. 'The community feeds them.' By poor people he meant people who were destitute, and he very clearly dissociated himself from this class.

The uncle we now went to see had a little booth outside the Mellah in which he sold silks. He was a small, thin man, pale and sad and of few words. His booth was unfrequented; no one came near it in all the time I was standing outside it. It looked as if all the passers-by went out of their way to avoid it. He answered my questions in correct but somewhat monosyllabic French. Business was very bad. Nobody was buying. They had no money. Foreigners no longer came because of the assassination attempts. He was a quiet man and assassination attempts were too loud for him. His lament was neither bitter nor vehement; he was one of those people who are always aware that alien ears may be listening to them, and his voice was so subdued that I could hardly understand him.

We left him as if we had never been there. I wanted to ask Élie how his uncle had behaved at the wedding. After all it had been only two days since the family had celebrated its great feast. I stifled this rather malicious remark, however, which in any case he would not have understood, and said that I must go back now. He accompanied me to the hotel. On the way he pointed out the clockmaker's where his brother worked. I peeped inside and saw him bent earnestly over a table studying watch components through a lens. Not wishing to disturb him, I walked on without drawing attention to myself.

Outside the hotel I stopped to say goodbye to Élie. His liberality with his relatives had given him fresh courage and he brought up the matter of the letter. 'I'll bring you the commandant's name,' he said ' – tomorrow.' 'Yes, yes,' I said, hurrying inside and looking forward to tomorrow.

From then on he appeared every day. If I was not there he walked round the block and came back. If I was still not there he stationed himself on the corner opposite the entrance to the hotel and waited patiently. On bolder days he took a seat in the hotel lobby. But he never sat there for more than a few minutes. He was shy of the hotel's Arab staff, who treated him with contempt, possibly recognizing him as a Jew.

He brought the commandant's name. But with it he brought all the documents he had ever possessed in his life. Not all at once; each day he came with one or two new ones that he had thought of in the meantime. He was evidently persuaded that I could draw up the desired injunction to the commandant of Ben Guérir perfectly well if I wanted to; and as to its effect once drawn up he entertained not the slightest doubt. There was an irresistible quality about papers that had a foreign name at the bottom. He brought me testimonials relating to the job he had had before; he really had worked briefly for the Americans as a 'plongeur'. He brought me testimonials regarding his younger brother, Simon. He never came without pulling a piece of paper from his pocket and holding it up in front of me. He would wait a little for the text to sink in and then suggest alterations to the letter I was to write to the commandant.

Meanwhile I had talked the whole business over very thoroughly with my American friend. He offered to recommend Élie Dahan to his compatriot himself, but he thought nothing of the young man's chances. He knew neither the commandant nor anyone else with a say in the allocation of jobs. But we were both reluctant to rob Élie of his hopes, and so the letter was written.

It was a relief to be able to greet him with this news and draw a piece of paper from my own pocket for a change.

'Read it to me,' he said suspiciously and a little brusquely.

I read him the English text from beginning to end, and although I knew he did not understand a word I read as slowly as possible.

'Translate it,' he said, his face a mask.

I translated it, lending a note of solemn emphasis to the French words. I handed him the letter. He looked for something and then examined the signature. The ink was not very dark and he shook his head.

'The commandant can't read that,' he said, handing the letter back, and without a trace of inhibition he added: 'Write me three letters. If the commandant does not send the letter back I will send the second one to another camp.'

'What do you need the third letter for?' I asked to hide my astonishment at his cheek.

'For me,' he said grandly.

I realized he wanted to add it to his collection, and the idea that it was this third letter that was most important to him forced itself upon me as irrefutable.

'Put your address,' he said then. The hotel was not

mentioned anywhere; obviously that was what he had been looking for.

'But there's no point,' I said. 'We're leaving soon. If anyone's going to answer the letter they need your address!'

'Put your address,' he said, unmoved. My objection had not made the slightest impression on him.

'All right, we can do that,' I said, 'but your address must be on there too – otherwise the whole thing's pointless.'

'No,' he said. 'Put the hotel.'

'But what will happen if they do want to give you the job? How will they get in touch with you? We're leaving next week and they certainly won't answer that quickly.'

'Put the hotel!'

'I'll tell my friend. Let's hope he won't be too annoyed at having to write the letter again.' I could not help punishing him for his obstinacy.

'Three letters,' was his reply. 'Put the hotel on all three letters.'

I sent him away peevishly and wished our paths need never cross again.

The next day he turned up wearing an air of particular solemnity and asked:

'Do you wish to meet my father?'

'Well, where is he?' I said.

'At the shop. He and my uncle have a shop. Two minutes from here.'

I accepted and we set off. It was in the modern street that led from my hotel to the Bab-Agenaou. I had been that way often, several times a day, and had cast many a glance into the shops to right and left. There were many

Jews among the shopkeepers and their faces were already familiar to me. Wondering whether one of them was his father, I mentally passed them in review. Which one could it be?

I had underestimated both the number and variety of those shops, however, because no sooner had I entered from the street than I was struck with astonishment that the one I was in had never caught my attention. It was stuffed full with sugar in every form, whether as sugar-loaves or in sacks. At every level and on every shelf around the shop there was nothing but sugar. I had never before seen a shop that sold nothing but sugar and I found it, God knows why, extremely amusing. The father was not there but the uncle was and I was introduced. He was an unpleasant little wisp of a man with a crafty face I would not have trusted an inch. He was dressed in the European style but his suit looked filthy and it was evident that the filth consisted of an unusual mixture of dust from the street and sugar.

The father was at no great distance and was sent for. Meanwhile, according to custom, peppermint tea was prepared for me. In view of the overwhelming sweetness potentially represented by my surroundings, however, the thought that I must drink some of it made me feel slightly sick. Élie explained in Arabic that I was from London. A gentleman in a European hat whom I had taken for a customer took a few steps towards me and said in English: 'I'm British.' He was a Jew from Gibraltar and his English was not at all bad. He wanted to know about my business and since I had nothing to tell him I served up the old story about the film again.

We talked a little and I sipped my tea. Then the father

arrived. He was a dignified man with a beautiful white
beard. He wore the skull-cap and robe of the Moroccan
Jew. He had a large, round head with a broad forehead,
but what I liked best about him was his laughing eyes.
Élie went and stood beside him and said with an implora-
tory gesture:

'Je vous présente mon père.'

I had never heard him say anything with so much
earnestness and conviction. 'Père' sounded positively
majestic in his mouth, and I would never have thought so
stupid a person capable of achieving such majesty. 'Père'
sounded like a lot more than 'American', and I was glad
that there was not much left of the commandant.

I shook the man's hand and looked into his laughing
eyes. He asked his son in Arabic where I was from and
what my name was. He could not speak a word of French,
so the son stood between us and with a zeal quite untypical
of him became our interpreter. He explained where I was
from and that I was a Jew, and he gave my name. The way
he said it, with his characterless voice and poor articu-
lation, it sounded like nothing.

'E-li-as Ca-ne-ti?' the father repeated on a note of
interrogation. He spoke the name aloud several times,
pronouncing each syllable distinctly and separately. In his
mouth the name became more substantial, more beautiful.
He looked not at me but straight ahead of him, as if the
name were more real than I and as if it were worth explor-
ing. I listened in amazement, deeply affected. In his sing-
song voice my name sounded to me as if it belonged to a
special language that I did not know. He weighed it mag-
nanimously four or five times; I thought I heard the clink
of weights. I felt no alarm, for he was not a judge. I

knew he would find my name's meaning and true mass; and when he had finished he looked up and his eyes laughed again into mine.

He was standing there as if he wanted to say: the name is good. But there was no language in which he could have told me. I read it in his face and experienced an overpowering surge of love for him. My boldest imaginings would never have pictured him like this. His dullard son and his crafty brother were both from another world. Only the watchmaker had inherited anything of his bearing, but he was not with us; there would have been no room for anyone else under all that sugar. Élie was waiting for me to say something for him to translate, but I could not. Awed, I remained perfectly silent. Perhaps I was also afraid of breaking the wonderful spell of the name-chanting. As a result we spent several long moments facing each other. If he only understands why I cannot speak, I thought; if my eyes could only laugh the way his do. It would have been a let-down to have entrusted anything more to that interpreter. As far as I was concerned *no* interpreter was good enough for him.

He waited patiently as I persisted in my silence. Finally an expression akin to mild irritation flitted across his brow and he spoke a sentence in Arabic to his son, who hesitated slightly before translating it for me.

'My father asks you to excuse him as he wishes to go now.'

I nodded and he shook me by the hand. He smiled, and the smile looked as if he now had to do something he did not enjoy doing; undoubtedly it was some kind of business deal. Then he turned from me and left the shop.

I waited for a few moments and then Élie and I went

out too. In the street I told him how much I had liked
his father.

'He is a great scholar,' he told me in tones of deep
respect, raising the outstretched fingers of his left hand
high into the air, where they remained hovering impres-
sively. 'He *reads* all night.'

From that day on Élie was home and dry with me. I
zealously fulfilled every one of his burdensome little wishes
because he was the son of that magnificent man. I felt
almost sorry for him for not having asked more, because
there was nothing I would not have done for him. He got
three English letters in which his zeal, his reliability and
honesty, indeed his indispensability when once employed
were all praised to high heaven. His younger brother
Simon, whom I had not even met, was no less competent
in other fields. Their Mellah address was not mentioned.

The name of our hotel stood resplendent at the head.
And all three letters were signed by my American friend in
black and very likely permanent ink. What is more, he
had added his home address in the States and even his passport number. When I went over this part of the letter
with Élie he could hardly believe his good fortune.

He brought me an invitation from his father to Purim:
would I care to celebrate the feast with him and his
family at home? I declined with cordial thanks. I could
imagine his father's disappointment at my ignorance of
the old customs. I would have got most of it wrong and
could only have said the prayers like a person who never
prays. It made me ashamed to face the old man, whom I
loved and wanted to spare this distress. Pleading work, I
brought myself to turn down the invitation and never see
him again. I am content to have seen him once.

Storytellers and scribes

The largest crowds are drawn by the storytellers. It is around them that people throng most densely and stay longest. Their performances are lengthy; an inner ring of listeners squat on the ground and it is some time before they get up again. Others, standing, form an outer ring; they, too, hardly move, spellbound by the storyteller's words and gestures. Sometimes two of them recite in turn. Their words come from farther off and hang longer in the air than those of ordinary people. I understand nothing and yet whenever I came within hearing I was rooted to the spot by the same fascination. They were words that held no meaning for me, hammered out with fire and impact: to the man who spoke them they were precious and he was proud of them. He arranged them in a rhythm that always struck me as highly personal. If he paused, what followed came out all the more forceful and exalted. I sensed the solemnity of certain words and the devious intent of others. Flattering compliments affected me as if they had been directed at myself; in perilous situations I was afraid. Everything was under control; the most powerful words flew precisely as far as the storyteller wished them to. The air above the listeners' heads was full of movement, and one who understood as little as I felt great things going on there.

In honour of their words the storytellers wore striking clothes. They were always dressed differently from their listeners. They favoured the more splendid materials; one or other of them always appeared in blue or brown velvet. They gave the impression of exalted yet somehow fairytale personages. They spared few glances for the people by whom they were surrounded. Their gaze was on their heroes, their characters. If their eye did fall on someone who just happened to be there it surely gave him an obscure feeling of being someone else. Foreigners were simply not there as far as they were concerned, did not belong in the world of their words. At first I refused to believe I was of so little interest to them; this was too unfamiliar to be true. So I stood there more than usually long, though I already felt the tug of other sounds in that place so replete with sounds – but they were still taking no notice of me when I was beginning to feel almost at home in the group of listeners. The storyteller had seen me, of course, but to him I was and remained an intruder in his magic circle: I did not understand him.

There were times when I would have given a great deal to be able to, and I hope the day will come when I can appreciate these itinerant storytellers as they deserve to be appreciated. But I was also glad I could not understand them. For me they remained an enclave of ancient, un-touched existence. Their language was as important to them as mine to me. Words were their nourishment, and they let no one seduce them into exchanging it for a better form of nourishment. I was proud of the power of storytelling that I witnessed them wielding over their linguistic fellows. I saw them as elder and better brothers to myself. In happy moments I told myself: I too can gather people round me to whom I tell stories; and they too listen to me. But instead of roaming from place to place never knowing whom I will find, whose ears will receive my story, instead of living in utter dependence on my story itself I have dedicated myself to paper. I live now behind the protection of desk and door, a craven dreamer, and they in the bustle of the marketplace, among a hundred strange faces that are different every day, unburdened by cold, superfluous knowledge, without books, ambition, or empty respectability. Having seldom felt at ease among the people of our zones whose life is literature – despising them because I despise something about myself, and I think that something is paper – I suddenly found myself here among authors I could look up to since there was not a line of theirs to be *read*.

But a little farther on in the same square I had to admit how seriously I had blasphemed against paper. Only a few steps from the storytellers the scribes had their pitch. It was very quiet here, the quietest part of the Djema el Fna. The scribes did nothing to recommend their skill. Delicate little men, they sat there in silence, their writing things in front of them, and never once gave you the impression they were waiting for clients. When they looked up they considered you with no particular curiosity, and their eyes soon travelled on to something else. Their benches were set up some distance apart, far enough for it to be impossible to hear from one to another. The more modest or possibly more conservative among them squatted on the ground. Here they cogitated or wrote in a confidential world apart, surrounded by the tumultuous din of the square and yet cut off from it. It was as if they were used to being consulted about secret complaints and, since this took place in public, had got into a certain habit of effacement. They themselves were barely present; all that counted here was the silent dignity of paper.

People came up to them singly or in pairs. Once I saw two veiled young women sitting on the bench before a

scribe, moving their lips almost imperceptibly as he nodded and almost as imperceptibly wrote. Another time I
noticed a whole family, extremely proud and respectable.
It consisted of four people, who had arranged themselves
on two benches at right angles with the scribe between
them. The father was an elderly, powerful-looking,
magnificently handsome Berber, experience and wisdom
plainly legible in his face. I tried to imagine a situation
in which he would be inadequate and could think of none.
Here he was, in his one and only inadequacy, his wife
beside him; her bearing was as impressive as his, for the
veil over her face left only the enormous dark eyes exposed,
and beside her on the bench sat two similarly-veiled
daughters. All four sat erect and extremely solemn.

The scribe, who was very much smaller, accepted their
respect. His features evinced a keen attentiveness, which
was as palpable as the prosperity and beauty of the family.
I watched them from only a short distance away without
hearing a sound or observing a single movement. The scribe
had not yet begun his actual business. He had probably
asked for and received an account of the matter and was
now considering how this could best be encompassed in
terms of the written word. The group gave such an impression of unity that its members might have known one
another for ever and occupied the same positions since the
beginning of time.

So intimately did they belong together that I did not
even ask myself what they had all come for, and it was not
until much later, when I had long left the square, that I
began to think about it. What on earth could it have been
that had required the whole family's attendance before
the scribe?

Choosing a loaf

In the evenings, after dark, I went to that part of the Djema el Fna where the women sold bread. They squatted on the ground in a long line, their faces so thoroughly veiled that you saw only their eyes. Each had a basket in front of her covered with a cloth, and on the cloth a number of flat, round loaves were laid out for sale. I walked very slowly down the line, looking at the women and their loaves. They were mature women for the most part, in shape not unlike the loaves. The smell of the loaves was in my nostrils, and simultaneously I caught the look of their dark eyes. Not one of the women missed me; they all saw me, a foreigner come to buy bread, but this I was careful not to do, wanting to walk right to the end of the row and needing a pretext for doing so.

Occasionally there was a young woman. The loaves looked too round for her, as if she had had nothing to do with their making. The young women's eyes were different too. None of the women, young or old, was long inactive. From time to time each would pick up a loaf of bread in her right hand, toss it a little way into the air, catch it again, tilt it to and fro a few times as if weighing it, give it a couple of audible pats, and then, these caresses completed, put it back on top of the other loaves. In this way the loaf itself, its freshness and weight and smell, as it were, offered themselves for sale. There was something naked and alluring about those loaves; the busy hands of women who were otherwise shrouded completely except for their eyes communicated it to them. 'Here, this I can give you of myself; take it in your hand, it comes from mine.'

There were men going past with bold looks in their eyes, and when one saw something that caught his fancy he stopped and accepted a loaf in his right hand. He tossed it a little way into the air, caught it again, tilted it to and fro a few times as if his hand had been a pair of scales, gave the loaf a couple of audible pats, and then, if he found it too light or misliked it for some other reason, put it back on top of the others. But sometimes he kept it, and you sensed the loaf's pride and the way it gave off a special smell. Slipping his left hand inside his robe, the man pulled out a tiny coin, barely visible beside the great shape of the loaf of bread, and tossed it to the woman. The loaf then disappeared under his robe – it was impossible to tell where it was any more – and the man went away.

The calumny

The beggar children's favourite pitch was near the 'Kutubiya' restaurant. This was where we all had our meals, midday and evening, so they knew we would not escape them. For the restaurant, which valued its reputation, the children constituted an undesirable adornment. When they came too close to the door they were driven away by the proprietor. They were better off stationing themselves on the corner opposite; we usually arrived for meals in small groups of three or four, and they could quickly surround us as soon as we hove in sight.

Some who had been in the city for months already were weary of giving and tried to shake the children off. Others hesitated before giving them something because they were ashamed of showing 'weakness' in front of their friends. After all, you had to learn to live here sometime, and the French inhabitants set a good or bad example, depending on how you looked at it, by never reaching into their pockets for a beggar on principle, even priding themselves on their thick-skinnedness. I was still fresh and as it were young in the city. I did not care what people thought of me. They could think me a fool if they wished – I loved the children.

If they happened to miss me I was miserable and sought them out myself without letting them see I was doing so. I liked their lively gestures, the tiny fingers they pointed into their mouths when with pitiful expressions they whined 'Manger! manger!', the unspeakably sad faces they pulled as if they really were on the verge of collapse from weakness and starvation. I liked their boisterous hilarity as soon as they had received something, the joyful eagerness with which they ran off, clutching their meagre booty, the incredible change in their faces: the dying now suddenly filled with bliss. I liked their little wiles, the way they brought babies up to me, holding their tiny, almost feelingless hands out towards me, begging 'for him too, for him too, manger! manger!' in order to double their alms. There were quite a lot of children; I tried to be fair, but of course I had my favourites among them, ones whose faces were so beautiful and so vivacious I would never have tired of looking at them. They followed me right to the restaurant door, feeling safe under my protection. They knew I was well-disposed towards them and they found it

tempting to get so close to that fabulous place that was
barred to them and where people ate so much.

The proprietor, a Frenchman with a round, bald head
and eyes like flypaper, who greeted his regulars with warm
and cordial glances, could not stand the beggar children
converging on his restaurant. Their rags were indelicate.
His well-dressed patrons should order their expensive food
in comfort without being constantly reminded of hunger
and lice. When I came in at the door and he happened to
be standing there and caught a glimpse of the horde of
children outside he shook his head in annoyance. But
since I belonged to a group of fifteen Englishmen who
every day without fail ate two meals in his restaurant, he
did not dare say anything to me but waited for a suitable
opportunity of dealing with the matter in a spirit of light-
hearted irony.

One noon, when it was stiflingly hot, the door of the
restaurant had been left open to admit some fresh air. I
and two of my friends, having survived the children's
onslaught, sat down at a free table near the open door.
The children could still see us and stayed where they were
outside, fairly close to the door. They wanted to pursue
their friendship with us and possibly also to see what we
were going to eat. They made signs to us and were particularly amused by our moustaches. One girl of perhaps
ten, the prettiest of them all, who had long been aware that
I had a soft spot for her, kept pointing to the tiny space
between her upper lip and her nose, grasping an imaginary
moustache between finger and thumb and pulling and
plucking at it vigorously. She laughed heartily as she did
so, and the other children laughed with her.

The proprietor came to our table to take our order and

saw the laughing children. Smiling broadly, he said to
me, 'Proper little tart, that one!' I was hurt by the insinua-
tion. Perhaps too I did not want to believe him, because I
was really fond of my beggar children. Innocently I asked,
'What – at that age? Surely not!'

'That's what you think,' he said. 'For fifty francs you
can have any one of them. They'll all go round the corner
with you just like that.'

I was most indignant and contradicted him vigorously.
'But that's impossible! It can't be true!'

'You don't know what goes on here,' he said. 'You ought
to see a bit of Marrakesh night life. I've lived here a long
time. When I first came here – that was during the war,
when I was still single' – he threw a brief but solemn
glance in the direction of his elderly wife, seated as always at the cash desk – 'I was with a couple of friends
and we had a good look round. One time we were taken
to a house and we'd hardly sat down before we were surrounded by a crowd of little girls, all nude. They squatted
at our feet and snuggled up to us from all sides, none of
them any bigger than that one out there and some of
them smaller.'

I shook my head in disbelief.

'There was nothing you couldn't have. We had a right
old time, and we had a lot of fun too. We played a splendid trick once, I must tell you about that. There were three
of us, me and two friends. One of us went to a *fatma* in
her room' – this was how the French contemptuously re-
ferred to native women – 'she wasn't a child, this one –
and we other two stood outside, looking into the room
through a hole. First he bargained with her for a long
time. Eventually they agreed on the price and he gave her

the money, which she put away in the bedside table. Then she turned the light out and the two of them lay down together. We'd seen all this from outside. As soon as it was dark one of us slipped into the room very quietly and crawled over to the bedside table. He carefully put his hand into the drawer and, while the others got on with their business, recovered the money. Then he crawled quickly out again and we both ran off. Soon afterwards our friend joined us. It meant he had been with the *fatma* for nothing, you see. You can imagine how we laughed! That was only one of the tricks we got up to.'

We were able to imagine it because he laughed uproariously now; he shook with laughter, his mouth pulled right open. We had not realized he had such a large mouth, never having seen him like this before. Usually he moved about his restaurant with a certain stateliness, decorously noting his privileged patrons' requirements with a reserve so total as to suggest that it was a matter of complete indifference to him what one ordered. The advice he gave was never obtrusive and invariably sounded as if it were given purely for the patron's benefit. Today, all reticence lost, he was rejoicing in his story. It must have been a marvellous time for him; and he did only one thing that called to mind his usual behaviour. In the middle of his narrative a small waiter approached our table. He curtly sent him off on an errand to prevent him from overhearing what he was telling us.

We, however, were doing an Anglo-Saxon freeze. My two friends, one of whom was a New Englander and the other an Englishman, and I, who had been living among them for fifteen years, shared the same feeling of abject disgust. We were a threesome too, we had it too good, and we may in some way have felt guilty on behalf of those other three who had joined forces to defraud a poor native woman of her earnings. He had told the story with beaming pride, seeing only the funny side of it, and his enthusiasm survived our sour smiles and embarrassed nods of acknowledgement.

The door was still open, the children still standing outside, expectant, patient. They sensed that they would not be driven away while his narrative lasted. I reminded myself that they could not understand him. He who had begun with such contempt for them had in a matter of minutes made himself contemptible. Whether what he was saying about them was a calumny or the truth, whatever the beggar children might do he was now far beneath them and I wished there really were a kind of punishment whereby he would have been dependent upon *their* intercession.

The donkey's concupiscence

I liked to return from my evening strolls through the streets of the city by way of the Djema el Fna. It was strange, crossing that great square as it lay almost empty. There were no acrobats any more and no dancers; no snake-charmers and no fire-eaters. A little man squatted forlornly on the ground, a basket of very small eggs before him and nothing and no one else anywhere near him. Acetylene lamps burned here and there; the square smelled of them. In the cookshops one or two men still sat over their soup. They looked lonely, as if they had nowhere to go. Around the edges of the square people were settling down to sleep. Some lay, though most squatted, and they had all pulled the hoods of their cloaks over their heads. Their sleep was motionless; you would never have suspected anything breathing beneath those dark hoods.

One night I saw a large, dense circle of people in the middle of the square, acetylene lamps illuminating them in the strangest way. They were all standing. The dark shadows on faces and figures, edged by the harsh light thrown on them by the lamps, gave them a cruel, sinister look. I could hear two native instruments playing and a man's voice addressing someone in vehement terms. I went up closer and found a gap through which I could see inside the circle. What I saw was a man, standing in the middle with a stick in his hand, urgently interrogating a donkey.

Of all the city's miserable donkeys, this was the most pitiful. His bones stuck out, he was completely starved, his coat was worn off, and he was clearly no longer capable of bearing the least little burden. One wondered how his legs still held him up. The man was engaged in a comic dialogue with him. He was trying to cajole him into something. The donkey remaining stubborn, he asked him questions; and when he refused to answer, the illuminated onlookers burst out laughing. Possibly it was a story in which a donkey played a part, because after a lengthy palaver the wretched animal began to turn very slowly to the music. The stick was still being brandished above him. The man was talking faster and faster, fairly ranting now in order to keep the donkey going, but it sounded to me from his words as if he too represented a figure of fun. The music played on and on and the men, who now never stopped laughing, had the look of man-eating or donkey-eating savages.

I stayed only a short time and so cannot say what happened subsequently. My repulsion outweighed my curiosity. I had long before conceived an affection for the donkeys of the city. Every step offered me occasion to feel indignant at the way they were treated, though of course there was nothing I could do. But never had quite such a lamentable specimen as this crossed my path, and on my way home I sought to console myself with the thought that he would certainly not last the night.

The next day was a Saturday and I went to the Djema el Fna early in the morning. Saturday was one of its busiest days. Onlookers, performers, baskets, and booths thronged the square; it was a job to make one's way through the crowd. I came to the place where the donkey had stood the evening before. I looked, and I could hardly believe my eyes: there he was again. He was standing all by himself. I examined him closely and there was no mistaking him; it was he. His master was nearby, chatting quietly with a few people. No circle had formed round them yet. The musicians were not there; the performance had not yet begun. The donkey was standing exactly as he had the night before. In the bright sunshine his coat looked even shabbier than at night. I found him older, more famished, and altogether more wretched.

Suddenly I became aware of someone behind me and of angry words in my ear, words I did not understand. Turning, I lost sight of the donkey for a moment. The man I had heard was pressed right up against me in the crowd, but it became apparent that he had been threatening someone else and not me. I turned back to the donkey.

He had not budged, but it was no longer the same donkey. Because between his back legs, slanting forwards and down, there hung all of a sudden a prodigious member. It was stouter than the stick the man had been threatening him with the night before. In the tiny space of time in which I had had my back turned an overwhelming change had come over him. I do not know what he had seen, heard, or smelled. But that pitiful, aged, feeble creature, who was on the verge of collapse and quite useless for anything any more except as the butt of comic dialogue, who was treated worse than a donkey in Marrakesh, that being, less than nothing, with no meat on his bones, no strength, no proper coat, still had so much lust in him that the mere sight absolved me of the impression caused by his misery. I often think of him. I remind myself how much of him was still there when I saw nothing left. I wish all the tormented his concupiscence in misery.

'Sheherazade'

She was the proprietress of a small French bar called the 'Sheherazade', the only bar in the Medina that was open all night. Sometimes it was quite empty; sometimes there were three or four people sitting in it. But when it was full, mostly between two and three in the morning, one heard every word the other patrons said, and one got into conversation with everybody. The place was tiny, you see, and as soon as twenty people were sitting or standing inside it looked as if the walls must burst apart.

Just around the corner was the empty square, the Djema el Fna, not ten paces from the bar. It is impossible to imagine a greater contrast. Around the square paupers

lay asleep in rags. Often they merged so closely with
their surroundings that one had to be careful not to bump
into them. Anybody in the square at that time of night
who was on his feet and walking was suspect and it was
best to be on one's guard against him. The life of the
Djema was long over by the time that of the little bar
began. Its frequenters looked European. It was used by
Frenchmen, Americans, English. It was used by Arabs
too; but they either wore European dress or they drank,
which was sufficient in itself to make them, at least in
their own eyes, modern and European. The drinks were
very expensive, and only well-to-do Arabs ventured inside the place. The people in rags who lay in the square had
nothing or a couple of francs in their pockets. Patrons of
the 'Sheherazade' paid fifty times that for a small brandy,
and they drank several in rapid succession. Those settling
down to sleep in the square were accustomed to Arab
music, with radios wailing noisily from every establishment
that boasted a roof over its customers' heads. In the 'Sheherazade' there was nothing but European dance music,
muted, and everyone who stepped inside felt a real swell.
Madame Mignon provided the latest hits. She was proud
of her records; about once a week she would come into the
bar with a fresh stack of records that she had just been
out to buy. She played them for her regulars and took a
lively interest in patrons' individual tastes.

   She had been born in Shanghai of a French father and
a Chinese mother. She had had her originally slit eyes
operated on, and now there was little of their Chinese
character left. She never made a secret of her Chinese
mother. She had lived in other French colonies before
coming to Morocco, including a number of years in Douala.

She had something against every nation; never have I come across such naive, unswerving prejudices as that woman had. But she would not hear a word against the French and the Chinese, always adding proudly, 'My mother was a Chinese. My father was a Frenchman.' She was as pleased with herself as she took exception to those of her customers whose origins differed from her own.

I gained her confidence as a result of a long conversation once when I was alone with her in the bar. Sometimes when my friends from the English film company had left without paying their rounds for the others, I would step in. This made her think I was wealthy; wealthy in a surreptitious way, as was the habit of Englishmen, who seldom showed it in their dress. Someone, possibly with the intention of pulling Madame Mignon's leg, had given out that I was a psychiatrist. As I frequently sat very still without saying a word and later, alone with her, questioned her at length about the patrons, she decided to credit the story. I did nothing to contradict it; it suited me, because then she told me more.

She was married to Monsieur Mignon, a tall, powerful fellow who had served in the Foreign Legion and gave her precious little help in her bar. When there were no patrons present he liked to sleep stretched out on the benches in the tiny room. But as soon as people came in whom he knew he took them round to the French brothel called the 'Riviera', which was only a few minutes' walk from the bar. He liked to spend an hour or two there and then come back, usually with his guests. They told his wife where they had been, reported on any new girls that had arrived at the brothel, had a drink, and later perhaps, taking other customers with them, went back to the

'Riviera'. It was the word one heard most often in the 'Sheherazade'.

Monsieur Mignon had a round, sleepy, boyish face above an abundance of shoulder. His smile was lazy, and for a Frenchman he spoke surprisingly slowly and little. His wife too could be silent; she was not without sensitivity and did not readily thrust herself forward. But once she had begun to talk she found it difficult to stop. Meanwhile he would rinse a few glasses or sleep or go to the 'Riviera'. Madame never allowed her powerful husband to throw out drunken patrons who became offensive. She took care of all that herself. It was her bar, and for dangerous cases she had a rubber truncheon hidden behind the counter, where the gramophone records were also kept. She took a delight in showing this truncheon to her friends, a performance that was invariably accompanied by suggestive laughter and by her saying, 'It's only for Americans'. Drunken Americans were her biggest problem, which qualified them too for her burning hatred. In her eyes there were two sorts of barbarian: natives and Americans.

Her husband had not always been in the Foreign Legion. One day he turned to me in his half indolent, half canny way and asked, 'You're a doctor, is that right, a doctor for the insane?' 'What makes you think that?' I asked, feigning surprise. 'We heard. I was in an insane asylum near Paris for two years. I was a warden.' 'Then you'll know something about it,' I said, and he felt flattered. He told me about his job as warden and how he had known his way around with the patients and been able to tell exactly which ones were dangerous and which not. He had had his own, simple classification for them, according to how dangerous they appeared to him. I questioned him about mad people in Marrakesh and he mentioned one or two locally notorious cases. From that evening on he treated me a little like a former superior in the same line of business. We used to exchange glances when someone in the bar was acting a bit insane; and now and then he would even offer me a brandy on the house.

Madame Mignon had a girl friend, just one, of whom she made extensive use. She was called Ginette and she came every night. Usually she sat on one of the high stools at the counter and waited. She was young and smartly dressed and of an extremely pale complexion, like someone who is up all night and sleeps during the day. She had protruding eyes, and every few moments she turned to the door of the bar to see whether someone was coming in, her eyes looking as if they were glued to the glass.

Ginette yearned for something to happen. She was twenty-two and had never been outside Morocco. She had been born here, of an English father who had gone to Dakar and did not give a damn about her, and an Italian mother. She liked to hear English spoken because it reminded her of her father. What he did, why he had been in Morocco and then gone to Dakar, I was never able to discover. Both Madame Mignon and she herself mentioned him occasionally with pride, and they suggested, without saying as much, that it had been on account of the daughter that he had disappeared. Undoubtedly they both wished it to be so, because with the father taking no interest in her whatsoever it was at least something that he should positively avoid the city in which she lived. The mother was never mentioned; I had the impression that she was

still living in Marrakesh, but she was not an object of
pride. Perhaps she was poor, or of a not particularly
honourable profession, or perhaps they did not think much
of Italians. Ginette dreamed of visiting England, about
which she was very curious. But she would have gone anywhere, even to Italy; she was waiting for a knight-errant
who would take her away from Morocco. During periods
when the bar was empty she seemed more than usually full
of expectation. The distance from her high stool to the
door was perhaps ten feet, but every time it opened she
shrank back as if her eyeballs had taken a blow.

Ginette was not alone when she first attracted my attention. She was sitting beside a very young, girlish-looking
man who was even more spruce than she was; his large,
dark eyes and brown complexion gave him away as
Moroccan. She was on very intimate terms with him and
they often came into the bar together. I took them for
lovers and used to watch them before I discovered anything about them. He always looked as if he had come
straight from the casino. Not only was he completely
French in the way he dressed; he let himself be caressed
by Ginette in public, which for an Arab was the height
of ignominy. They drank a great deal. Sometimes they
had a third person with them, a man of perhaps thirty
who seemed rather more masculine and was not quite so
dolled-up.

The first time Ginette addressed me – rather shyly,
since she took me for an Englishman – she was sitting at
the counter; I was sitting on her right, and her young man
was on the other side. She asked how the film was getting
on that my friends were making in Marrakesh. For her
this was no small event, and as I soon became aware she

would have given her life to be in the film. I answered
her questions politely. Madame Mignon was delighted that
we had finally come together, her best friend and myself.
We talked for a while, then she introduced the young man
on her left: he was her husband. This surprised me; it
was the last thing I would have thought of. They had been
living together for a year already. As a couple they gave
the impression of being still on their honeymoon. But
when Ginette was sitting there without him she kept looking longingly at the door, and it was by no means her husband's presence she yearned for. I questioned them in a
tactful, joking way about their life and learned that they
left the bar at three and went home to eat supper. Around
five o'clock in the morning they went to bed, and they
slept through until the afternoon.

What did her husband do for a living? I wanted to
know. 'Nothing,' she said, 'he has his father.' Madame
Mignon, who was listening, greeted this information with
a malicious smile. The brown, girlish-looking man smiled
bashfully, while still managing to show a good deal of his
beautiful teeth. His vanity eclipsed everything, even the
most painful embarrassment. We drank each other's
health and got into conversation. I realized that he was as
spoiled as he looked. I asked him how much time he had
spent in France. He seemed so thoroughly French. 'None,'
he said. 'I've never been outside Morocco.' Would he have
liked to go to Paris? No, he didn't think so. Would he
have liked to visit England? No, not really. Was there
anywhere he would have liked to go? No. His answers
were without exception feeble, as if he had no real will.
I sensed there must be something else that he was not
talking about, something that tied him to this place. It

cannot have been Ginette, because she made it quite clear that she would rather have been anywhere else but here.

The couple, apparently so smooth and ordinary, were a riddle to me. I saw them every night in the little bar. Apart from such strangers as came into the bar they were interested in one thing: Madame Mignon's record collection. They requested particular songs; some they found so beautiful that they were played six times in succession. Then, the music getting to them, they would begin to dance in the tiny space between counter and door. They pressed their limbs together so tightly that it was a little embarrassing to watch them. Ginette enjoyed this highly intimate style of dancing, but for the onlookers' sakes she would complain about her husband: 'It's terrible with him. He won't dance any other way. I've told him time and time again. He says he can't help it.' Then the next dance began, and once they were dancing she was meticulous about not missing a single spin of the disc. I pictured Ginette in another country, wherever her fancy took her, and how she would lead exactly the same life there, with the same people, at the same time, and I saw her in London dancing to the same records.

One night when I was alone in the bar Madame Mignon asked me how I liked Ginette. Knowing what was expected of me, I said, 'She's a very pleasant girl.'

'She's unrecognizable!' said Madame Mignon. 'If you knew how she'd changed in the last year! She's miserable, the poor thing! She should never have married him. These natives are all rotten husbands. His father's wealthy, he comes of a good family, it's true, but he disinherited him when he married Ginette. And her father doesn't want to know about her now that she's married an Arab. So they both have nothing.'

'How do they manage, then, if he doesn't work and his father gives him nothing?'

'You don't know? Don't you know who his friend is?'

'No, how should I?'

'But you've seen him sitting in here with them. His friend is one of the Glaoui's sons. He's his favourite. It's been going on for a long time. Now the Glaoui's angry with his son. He has nothing against women. He's all for his sons' having as many women as they want. But not men — he doesn't like that. A few days ago he sent his son away.'

'And Ginette's husband lived from that?'

'Yes. And from her too. He makes her sleep with wealthy Arabs. There's one particularly, at the court of the Glaoui's son, who likes Ginette. He's not young any more but he's rich. She wouldn't have him at first but her husband forced her. Now she's got used to him. Now the three of them often sleep together. Her husband beats her if she refuses. But that's only with others now — he's very jealous. He'll only let her sleep with men who pay for it. He throws jealous scenes in front of her when there's someone she likes. He beats her when there's one she doesn't like and won't have even for money, and he beats her when there's one she likes so much she'd sleep with him without the money. That's why she's so miserable. The poor girl can never do what she wants. She's waiting for a man who'll take her away from here. It's my wish for her that she does get away — I feel sorry for her. At the same time she's my only friend here. If she goes I'll have nobody.'

'You say the Glaoui is angry with his son?'

'Yes, he's sent him away for a while. He hopes that he'll
forget his darling. But he won't forget him – they're so
wrapped up in each other.'

'And Ginette's friend?'

'He's gone too. He had to go with the Glaoui's son.
He's a member of his court.'

'So now they're both away?'

'Yes. It's a terrible blow for her. Now they have no
money. They must be living on credit. But it won't be for
long. It's not the first time the Glaoui has tried to separate
them. The son always comes back. He can't stand it.
Being without Ginette's husband for any length of time is
more than he can stand. A few weeks and he's back again,
and his father gives in.'

'So everything will be all right again.'

'Oh, it'll sort itself out, yes – it's nothing serious. It
makes him a bit short with her, that's all. He's trying to
find someone to fill the gap. That's why he talked to you.
They say you're very rich. He was thinking of himself
at first but I told him there was nothing doing there.
You're much too good for him to my mind. Do you like
Ginette?'

Only now did I begin to grasp that the rumour of my
wealth had rebounded on me. In one respect, however, I
was doing Madame Mignon an injustice.

'Someone ought to take her away from here,' she said.
'Don't give him any money for Ginette. It goes as it comes,
and the poor girl is no better off. She'll never manage
to save anything with him. He takes it all off her. Just
go away with her. She told me: she's willing if you are.
He can't get away. He belongs to the Glaoui's son's court,

you see, so he can't simply leave just like that. He'd never get a passport. I feel so sorry for the girl. She looks worse and worse every day. You should have seen her a year ago – so fresh she was, like a rosebud. She needs good care and a decent life. After all she's an Englishwoman. Of course she is – her father was English. And yet she's so sweet. You'd hardly believe it. Would you have taken her for an Englishwoman?'

'No,' I said. 'Or perhaps I would. Perhaps I would have known she was English from her refinement.'

'Right,' said Madame Mignon. 'She does have a sort of refinement, doesn't she? Like an Englishwoman. Personally I don't like the English. They're too quiet for me. Look at your friends! There can be seven, eight of them sitting there the whole evening, for hours on end, and you don't hear a word. It gives me the creeps. You never know if you haven't got a latent sex murderer. But compared to Americans – them I can't stand at all. They're barbarians, they are. Have you seen my rubber truncheon?' She took it out from behind the counter and swung it to and fro a couple of times. 'I keep it for Americans. It's often come in handy, believe me!'

The unseen

At twilight I went to the great square in the middle of the city, and what I sought there were not its colour and bustle, those I was familiar with, I sought a small, brown bundle on the ground consisting not even of a voice but of a single sound. This was a deep, long-drawn-out, buzzing 'e-e-e-e-e-e-e-'. It did not diminish, it did not increase, it just went on and on; beneath all the thousands of calls and cries in the square it was always audible. It was the most unchanging sound in the Djema el Fna, remaining the same all evening and from evening to evening.

While still a long way off I was already listening for it. A restlessness drove me there that I cannot satisfactorily explain. I would have gone to the square in any case, there was so much there to attract me; nor did I ever doubt I would find it each time, with all that went with it. Only for this voice, reduced to a single sound, did I feel something akin to fear. It was at the very edge of the living; the life that engendered it consisted of nothing but that sound. Listening greedily, anxiously, I invariably reached a point in my walk, in exactly the same place, where I suddenly became aware of it like the buzzing of an insect:

'e-e-e-e-e-e-e-'

I felt a mysterious calm spread through my body, and whereas my steps had been hesitant and uncertain hitherto I now, all of a sudden, made determinedly for the sound. I knew where it came from. I knew the small, brown bundle on the ground, of which I had never seen anything more than a piece of dark, coarse cloth. I had never seen the mouth from which the 'e-e-e-e-e-' issued; nor the eye; nor the cheek; nor any part of the face. I could not have said whether it was the face of a blind man or whether it could see. The brown, soiled cloth was pulled right down over the head like a hood, concealing everything. The creature – as it must have been – squatted on the ground, its back arched under the material. There was not much of the creature there, it seemed slight and feeble, that was all one could conjecture. I had no idea how tall it was because I had never seen it standing. What there was of it on the ground kept so low that one would have stumbled over it quite unsuspectingly, had the sound ever stopped. I never saw it come, I never saw it go; I do not know whether it was brought and put down there or whether it walked there by itself.

The place it had chosen was by no means sheltered. It was the most open part of the square and there was an incessant coming and going on all sides of the little brown heap. On busy evenings it disappeared completely behind people's legs, and although I knew exactly where it was and could always hear the voice I had difficulty in finding it. But then the people dispersed, and it was still in its place when all around it, far and wide, the square was empty. Then it lay there in the darkness like an old and very dirty garment that someone had wanted to get rid of and had surreptitiously dropped in the midst of all the people where no one would notice. Now, however, the people had dispersed and only the bundle lay there. I never waited until it got up or was fetched. I slunk away in the darkness with a choking feeling of helplessness and pride.

The helplessness was in regard to myself. I sensed that I would never do anything to discover the bundle's secret. I had a dread of its shape; and since I could give it no other I left it lying there on the ground. When I was getting close I took care not to bump into it, as if I might hurt or endanger it. It was there every evening, and every evening my heart stood still when I first distinguished the sound, and it stood still again when I caught sight of the bundle. How it got there and how it got away again were matters more sacred to me than my own movements. I never spied on it and I do not know where it disappeared

to for the rest of the night and the following day. It was
something apart, and perhaps it saw itself as such. I was
sometimes tempted to touch the brown hood very lightly
with one finger – the creature was bound to notice, and
perhaps it had a second sound with which it would have
responded. But this temptation always succumbed swiftly
to my helplessness.

I have said that another feeling choked me as I slunk
away: pride. I was proud of the bundle because it was
alive. What it thought to itself as it breathed down there,
far below other people, I shall never know. The meaning
of its call remained as obscure to me as its whole existence:
but it was alive, and every day at the same time, there it
was. I never saw it pick up the coins that people threw it;
they did not throw many, there were never more than two
or three coins lying there. Perhaps it had no arms with
which to reach for the coins. Perhaps it had no tongue with
which to form the 'l' of 'Allah' and to it the name of God
was abbreviated to 'e-e-e-e-e'. But it was alive, and with
a diligence and persistence that were unparalleled it uttered
its one sound, uttered it hour after hour, until it was the
only sound in the whole enormous square, the sound that
outlived all others.